This book
belongs to:

This is a Carlton Book

Text copyright © 1999 Joseph Corré and Serena Rees
Design copyright © Carlton Books

This edition published by Carlton Books Limited 1999
20-22 Mortimer Street
London W1N 7RD

A CIP catalogue for this book is available from the British Library.

ISBN 1 85868 758 6

Printed and bound in Spain

Senior Executive Editor: Venetia Penfold
Design Manager: Penny Stock
Editor: Lisa Dyer
Design concept and layout: Kim Le Liboux
Picture researcher: Alex Pepper
Production: Alexia Turner

Agent Provocateur

A CELEBRATION OF FEMININITY

Joseph Corré and Serena Rees

WITH PRIA TANEJA

CARLTON

Contents

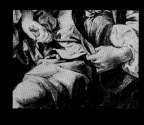

At a time when political correctness has created an anti-individual environment to avoid offending anyone and when companies only act upon ideas after the approval of marketing men, the aptly named Agent Provocateur was created to redress the balance. In a democracy where your only real choice is where you spend your money ('I shop therefore I am'), we found it necessary to open an outlet that we could use as a platform for our ideas and where we could provokingly display the sexuality of the female form without embarrassment or shame.

Of all the obsessions that have dominated the world of art, literature, fashion and even politics, the female form is one that still continues to fascinate us, along with the primitive desire to attract and the devices used to do so. In this book we are able to go deeper and into more detail about our ideas and explore them with you. The process has forced us to consider our raison d'être, by unravelling our ideas and thoughts and then answering, one by one, the questions they raised. The difficulty was to clearly communicate what we found through text and to convey to the reader the same sense of enthusiasm we had. These qualities, and more, are embodied in great writers, which we do not claim to be. However, what we can claim is that, within this work, we have been honest and looked deeply at all the statements we have made before allowing their inclusion. With no desire to simply fill space, we have treated each page as something special, something precious.

Introduction

This book is about many things: history, politics, culture and sexuality. Each chapter and parts of them could easily have been lengthy books in their own right. We begin the book by exploring historical changes in attitudes towards femininity. We look at the silhouette of the female form and how underwear has developed and embedded the form within our psyche. We discuss design and construction, giving a brief history of the relationship between lingerie and fashion. The chapters on fantasy and striptease are designed to provoke the imagination and, hopefully, lead to exciting adventures.

There have been moments when we have been plagued with anxiety about missing things out or not exploring certain ideas more fully - especially as we were refused permission to reproduce certain significant images. However, we hope that you will find the book stimulating, raising all the questions in your own mind which we have left there on purpose for you.

Joseph + Serena

Chapter 1 Femininity

The term 'feminine' has meant many different things throughout time, from pretty-looking women, to motherly types who were good at domestic chores, to those who excelled at flirting but not much else. Halfway through the twentieth century the feminist movement became a serious force, but with it came confusion about what being feminine really meant.

At the end of the century, femininity is flaunted, encouraged and enjoyed by women who rejoice in their utter difference from men. In this chapter we invite you to discover your own ideal of femininity among the diverse representations that are explored.

This is not meant to be a chronological overview of every significant event in terms of femininity, but simply a few pertinent examples that we hope will stimulate you and create an exciting atmosphere.

Though the image and symbolism of the female body have gone through many incarnations, the prevalent themes of softness, delicacy and mystery, to mention but a few, resurface again and again, suggesting that those qualities considered quintessentially feminine are perhaps those which represent certain truths about the female body. If you chart the history of fashion, particularly of the past one hundred years, every attempt to de-feminize the female figure has resulted in a strong call for the revival of femininity embodied in these qualities.

The very nature of the female body has meant that over the years parts of it have been sexualized or de-sexualized and coupled with varied meanings incongruent from one era to the next. Consider the thin muslin chemises worn by French and English women over breast-lifting corsets in the late 1700s, or the Empire line, low-cut and flimsy, more than half a century before Victorian prudery dictated that any glimpse of flesh was too revealing. The Victorians insisted that even the legs of tables should be covered by a ridiculously long cloth, just in case any man found them too arousing! This kind of puritanism has always tried to conceal the delights of the female body and is still concerned with maintaining the subjugation of women by controlling their self expression – why do those Muslim women wear head-to-toe hijab? Though women are complicit, it is this puritanical sensibility that has constantly hampered the definition of the female body as truly pure, insisting on hiding it away like something to be ashamed of. Why this fear of honest expression?

12

Opposite: Bettina Rheims, CHAMBRE CLOSE, 7 November, Paris.

GODDESS

Throughout history, eroticism and the idealization of the feminine form have been explicitly realized in mythic tradition and artistic expression. The pagans visualized their goddess as a fertile, all-powerful woman with flowing locks and bared breasts. Ancient civilizations had many such goddesses, for example the Roman virgin-huntress Diana or the Greek Hecate. The Greeks' aesthetic was the beauty and harmony of the body, so limbs were perfectly proportioned and breasts were round and firm. Other ideals of femininity were represented by goddesses such as Isis, Psyche, and the Muses and the Fates, to mention but a few. In this tradition, everything had its natural place and was given the importance it deserved, including sexual life. Unpolluted by the false shame brought about by religion, sex and eroticism had an accepted position in social and celestial life; for example, Venus watched over romantic lovers while her mother Dionysia patronized orgiastic revellers. The mythologies of these ancient civilizations record their goddesses as taking lovers and husbands, having adulterous affairs or being emblems of the purest virginity.

Above: With charming innocence, a lady's hand seeks for pleasure.

ART AND THE IMAGE OF WOMEN

This freedom of expression in classical mythology inspired the Renaissance painters and sculptors after the Dark Ages. They were interested in showing life without the distorting lens of rigid morality, so in a way the Renaissance culture, which celebrated the joy and purity of the body, was a rebirth of pagan ideals about sexuality. Through the poses of the artistic 'nude' the naked body was legitimized and, consequently, the nude was almost a subterfuge for the representation of feminine eroticism.

As a starting point, consider the provocation of a direct look from a woman, the invitation to become a voyeur. It is no coincidence that the first grave offence for orthodox women of all persuasions is to look a man straight in the eye. Two interesting examples are Titian's VENUS OF URBINO and Goya's MAJA.

The looks that these two women give represent the lack of fear or inhibition they have about their bodies. This idea itself might be considered a major theme in discussing attitudes towards female eroticism. Far from wantonly offering herself to the lascivious gropings of random watchers, Maja's direct look seems to say, 'admire me, admire my body. I know it is beautiful; it is ready for pleasure.' It is the Maja's knowledge of the sensations of pleasure that makes the painting so subversive. Interestingly, Goya's painting had a clothed version on a sliding frame that could be moved aside to reveal the nude. Titian's Venus, who gently touches herself with an arch, provocative look on her face, seems to be inviting the viewer to watch her pleasure – the perfect voyeuristic fantasy.

Continuing in this tradition is a painting of a woman in the time of Charles II. She is dressed in her chemise, and has pulled off the bed sheet and draped it over her shoulder. At first sight she looks like a classic Greek sculpture, but this was a mere ploy to legitimize the fact that she could be admired in her underwear, ready for bed. This subterfuge is emblematic of the attitudes that have surrounded the depiction of the female body until the early part of the twentieth century, so that even looking at what was ostensibly 'high art' contained a frisson of the forbidden.

There is a story about a young girl in the 1700s, the daughter of a French courtier. The onset of puberty was considered the coming of age for a young woman and to celebrate this, her father proudly displayed her at church, breasts bared and nipples rouged. Far from causing an outrage, she was considered sweet, expressive and feminine. It is a scene of pagan initiation, where the father's 'display' of her indicates a homage to her emerging womanhood and sexuality. The focus on the breasts, in particular, illustrates a pure admiration of her feminine attributes. Can you imagine the uproar if Prince Andrew took his daughter to their local church service with her breasts so provocatively displayed? He would be labelled disgusting and sacrilegious, especially with twentieth-century obsessions and paranoias about youth and sexuality. What

16

Right: Titian's Venus of Urbino.

Opposite: Goya's Maja Unclothed, pictured here, was covered by Maja Clothed on a sliding frame that could be moved aside to reveal the nude version.

ADMIRE ME, ADMIRE
my body.
I KNOW IT
is beautiful:
IT IS
ready for pleasure.

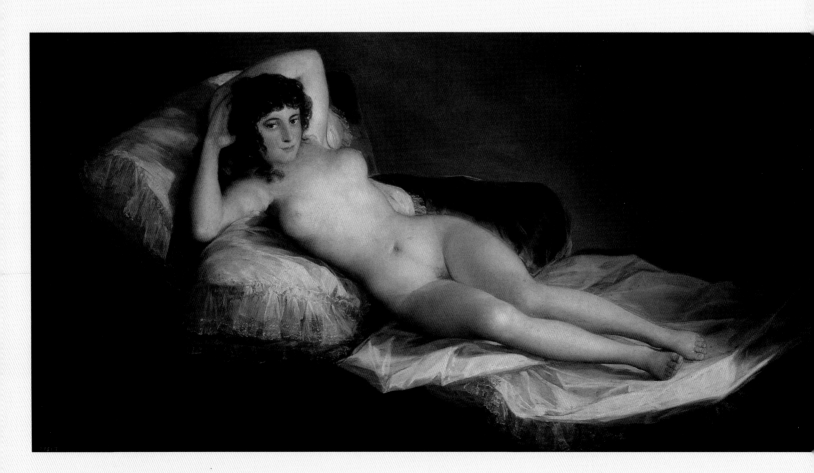

is also interesting about this story is that a pure fantasy enactment such as this was condoned simply because it was exciting to the participants. Another example is the famous story of Marie Antoinette playing at being a shepherdess in Versailles, with elaborate costumes and well-behaved sheep. This extravagance would ultimately lead to the downfall of the aristocracy, but the freedom of expression and absolute indulgence of fantasies is quite exhilarating to imagine.

The eighteenth-century painter François Boucher is well known for his romantic expression. One of his most interesting and erotic works is of a girl aged about 14. She does not look at us. She is pliant, naked and waiting, and her pose and the ornamentation of her body suggest knowledge and, indeed, readiness for sex. The parallel with her counterpart, the courtier's daughter, exists in their similar ages and in their representation of the attitudes of the French Court at that time. The upper classes condoned the exhibitionism of the courtier's daughter, with its spiritual overtone, and Boucher's scandalous juvenile was actually the mistress of King Louis XV.

Boucher's painting of the nude girl has since been an inspiration to the likes of Helmut Newton (ROSELYNE ON NAPOLEON'S BED, Paris, 1975) and Mel Ramos (TOUCHE BOUCHER, 1973), among others, because it is so erotic. However neither of these photographs, nor the numerous fashion shoots that have also celebrated the pose, have been able to capture the magic of the original painting. No matter how many times it is emulated, the relationship between Boucher and his model remains unique. She looks completely confident, utterly sexy and electric. She and Boucher were in perfect communication and thus, through his genius, we have been left with an image that is eternally exciting.

In Delacroix's painting, Liberty Leading the People (1830), a young peasant woman stands at the head of her compatriots, holding the French Tricolour. Her breasts are exposed, and at her feet a young man kneels adoringly. In front of her, another man points a long rifle at her breast. The strength of this imagery lies undeniably in the fact that the ideal of freedom is represented by her nakedness - the breast does not invite one to fondle, but to worship. Why the breast instead of, say, a penis or a man of arms? Of course, the political reason is that corsets were the apparel of the upper classes, the aristocracy that was overthrown. However, the breast as an object of profound beauty does not intimidate with connotations of violence. Instead, it has the power to move us deeply, to leave us awestruck even as we recognize that this breast is the one we suckled at, the breast we love to caress or have caressed.

These paintings introduce the notion of change that we find interesting, specifically the change that occurs dramatically, that causes controversy and redefines attitudes towards the feminine form. Far from claiming any position as authorities on art history or culture, we use these examples to form a picture of certain transformations in social attitudes towards women, and also to raise questions in our minds as to how they fit in with our idea of femininity. Instead of being gradual or systematic, these changes have actually been quite abrupt, and even conflicting, as society has been influenced by events and other cultures and has diversified from the puritan model that has held, and indeed still holds, much of the world in its grasp.

19

Left: The magic quality of La Petite Morphée by François Boucher.

Overleaf: Helmut Newton's Roselyne on Napoleon's Bed, Paris, 1975.

Right: Eugène Delacroix's triumphant LIBERTY LEADING THE PEOPLE. 1830.

Below: Gustave Coubert flaunted the taboo against depicting female genitalia with his emphatically erotic painting, THE ORIGIN OF THE WORLD. 1866.

The repression of sexuality, especially female sexuality, has been enforced by organized religion since its inception. Christianity and other religions have played a decisive role in unnaturally redefining how people should behave, and it is religion that has had the most powerful effect in altering people's attitudes towards their sexuality. Over centuries of indoctrination, sex and the female body became dirty, something to be concealed and ashamed of, instead of being the most natural and pleasurable of creations. How many people have been killed for their sexual expression because of the dictates of one religion or another?

Even today stories of Muslim women being stoned or beaten to death because of real or supposed sexual experiences are far from unheard of. It is this orthodoxy which caused women to be labelled harlots and whores if they showed the slightest interest in sexual life through their clothes or behaviour.

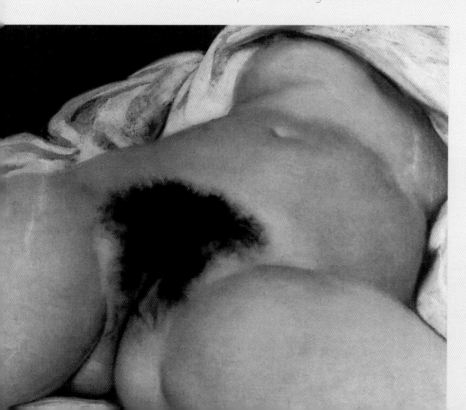

CHEESECAKE AND WHIPLASH

A good place to pick up this exploration is the 1950s because the decade is so rich in imageries of the feminine and the erotic and is notorious for its excessive domestication of women.

We are all familiar with the 'I Love Lucy' housewife with her hourglass figure and nuclear family, always making perfect pies, but the erotic side of this image is the glorious pin-up girl – the luscious but chaste 'cheesecakes' of Gil Elvgren and Harry Ekman. The pin-up girls invariably found themselves in risqué situations with their pink silk knickers around their ankles. These women were glowingly lovely, but they also conspired to enforce the idea that femininity equalled stupidity.

Seemingly, women were in a kind of role-play situation: their men wanted women who were homebound and maternal, yet able to look like, and slip into, the role of the pretty, dumb, ultimately acquiescent pin-up. It could be said that the 1950s pin-ups were catering to a solely male-inspired fantasy of what women should look like; however, women such as Zoe Mozert, who often used herself as a model, were among the most talented illustrators of the time. Another, perhaps better-known example is the pin-up legend Betty Page. Of all the women who were photographed as pin-ups, hers is the only image that has become a timeless symbol of feminine power and sexual freedom.

Discovered on a beach when she was 27, Betty started modelling as a pin-up and went on to become Irving Klaw's most popular bondage model. After her disappearance from public life in 1957, she gained a cult following.

Her photographs capture the reality of feminine sexuality because she is totally natural in front of the camera, never fake but just genuinely happy and sexy. Betty's visible enthusiasm is electric, whether she was tied up and being spanked or posing on the beach. Her photographs do not make her into a sex object. On the contrary, she is in complete control and always looks as if she is enjoying herself. Betty was unique in that she loved her work and had no hang-ups about sexuality. She designed and made her own bikinis and costumes for different assignments, from amateur photography clubs to bondage modelling stints, without any 'superstar' ego because she was just trying to do the best job she could. She never thought that fetish and bondage modelling was wrong or vulgar, nor at the time did she see herself as a pioneer of female sexual expression. She was simply being herself. This honesty is what makes her so interesting. In an age of conformity and bottle blondes, Betty was a free spirit who simply did what she enjoyed and never presented a manufactured image of sex, only what was real.

The pin-up explosion must be considered in the context of what is called the 'American Dream' and the influence of Hollywood in perpetuating and directing this myth of national solidarity and prosperity. The all-pervasive influence of the silver screen had a profound affect on the way American, and indeed European, women saw themselves.

The desire to emulate was strong and there was no ethos of individuality in appearance, a fact that has been consistently parodied about this period. The whole point of the American Dream was that everyone believed in it, and along with it, the precept of the beautiful but dumb woman. Two world wars contributed significantly to the liberation of women in the professional sphere, but this was a direct threat to the vision of masculine America. So Hollywood and the pin-up stepped in to grip the imagination of America and Europe en masse by promoting this excessively feminine fantasy girl and letting her form their ideas about what a woman should be.

Left: Betty Page by Leone Frollo. Called 'the artist who loves women', Frollo's stylish and sophisticated women are playful and uninhibited no matter what their predicament, whether submitting to or controlling exquisite sexual games.

The fabulous Betty Page: discovered on a beach when she was 27. Betty started modelling as a pin-up and went on to become Irving Klaw's most popular bondage model.

Her photographs capture the reality of feminine sexuality because she is totally natural in front of the camera, never fake but just genuinely happy and sexy.

4652

CHICKS and CHUCKLES

OCTOBER 1955

15¢

Betty Page

What better icon of femininity to prove this point than Marilyn Monroe - she was a created woman from her pose to her clothes, a version of femininity orchestrated by those who controlled her. What elevated her to the status of idol even in her own lifetime, was the desire created inside women to be like her, or more specifically, to look like her. Yes, she was a manufactured image, but that did not prevent her from becoming the most idolized woman in Western history.

Marilyn and her contemporaries may have fuelled the sexual fantasies of millions of men, but there is a flip side, what some may call a dark side, to this apple pie image: whips, chains and lots of leather - the age-old combination of pain and pleasure that has obsessed Western eroticism for hundreds of years. Sado-masochism derives its name from VENUS IN FURS author Leopold von Sacher-Masoch and the notorious Marquis de Sade, but of course as a practice has been indulged in for much longer.

Perhaps the influence of the Christian/Puritan tradition awakened the impulse to be punished for sexual pleasure, or perhaps it is a psychological trait inherent in all of us to one degree or another. Whether someone is simply obeying your spoken command, or you are tying another up, the power of knowing they will let you do whatever you want to them, is a heady aphrodisiac. If anything, the existence of this dark side emphasizes the fact that it is impossible to put boundaries on sexuality. However hard a sanitized, safe version of sexuality is promoted, the individuality that characterizes true sexual expression cannot be repressed.

Men such as Irving Klaw, in his famed studios with models like Betty Page and stripper Tempest Storm, promoted this dark side of sexuality. With his sister Paula, Klaw ran Movie Star News, a shop that sold publicity and photographs of the popular film stars of the day. Due to demand, he set up a studio on the second floor of his building on 14th Street, New York City, to take photographs of girls in lingerie and bondage gear. The photographs would then be sold by mail order or illicitly under the counter because of censorship laws.

Klaw was paranoid about being shut down and insisted on the decency of his models, often making them wear two pairs of underwear if he thought the underwear was transparent. Paula was the one who would tie and truss the models up, allowing no one else to touch them, and the studio became a magnet for artists, film-makers and photographers, including Eric Stanton, one-time protégé of the inimitable John Willie.

Willie, the black sheep of the Coutts banking family, was the creator of damsels in distress who appeared in his magazine BIZARRE (1946-1956). His wicked beauties, such as Gwendoline and the Countess, with their immaculate corsetry and eight-inch heels, epitomized the fetish figure. Willie included all the main elements of fetishism in his drawings and cartoons. His characters practise the obsessive, repetitive, yet playful rituals that allow the most transgressive sexual inventions. He explored the isolation and objectification of a single part - the feet, for example. And, lastly, he depicted the regalia of shining corsets and waspies cinching waists into impossible spans, outrageous high heels, the symbolic whips and plenty of good old-fashioned rope. The real brilliance of the cartoons lies in their impossibility. Willie and Stanton never limited their imagination and so their characters contort themselves into the most outrageous bondage positions, pushing the boundaries of sexual fantasy.

One could say that what is condemned as male mental perversion and as an instigation to violence over women may instead be considered as an ode to femininity, an exaltation of it, even though expressed in unusual terms.

His world is the world of the true fetish – objects and psychology, the visual language of the fetish.

Stefano Piselli and Riccardo Morrochi, eds.,

THE ART OF JOHN WILLIE: SOPHISTICATED BONDAGE, BOOK ONE

The ideas of submission and domination, the threat of violence and pain, are the imagistic opposite of the Vargas girl. Whereas the pin-up was a manufactured aesthetic of femininity, meant to captivate everyone who saw her, the fact is that sexuality will manifest itself in all its diversity. To force a belief or representation of sexuality on to anyone else is impossible. That which we find erotic is completely specific to ourselves, at the very core of our natures, complex and immutable. In the same way, John Willie's drawings, though now relatively well known, were the result of a private passion, and this is what makes him so interesting. If the pin-up was a mass experience, then Willie's work was the intensely private personal experience born of an all-consuming belief in a vision of sexuality that he wanted to share.

THE END OF TEASE

Though the popularity of the pin-up continued well into the 1960s, the new decade saw a reaction to all oppressive systems of so-called 'normal' life as practised in post-war Western society, 'normal' meaning the morally righteous stereotype of the nuclear family with a working father, housebound mother and two children. Normality was essentially conforming to a mainstream life: white, middle-class, suburban, safe. Girls were expected to be excellent homemakers, wives and mothers, and above all, during their teenage years they were expected to be chaste.

Towards the end of the 1950s, rebellion became a byword for a new generation, as existing values were challenged for their narrow and restrictive view of life. Change was pervasive and dramatic, not only in America where the 1960s would see the onset of the Civil Rights movement and the Vietnam crisis, but also in Europe. The Baader-Meinhof gang, operating in a partitioned Germany, is a prime example of the kind of changes taking place: extreme, violent and cataclysmic. This generation of youth, whose parents had lost a war and had returned to change nothing, were determined to instigate a mass social change through the most notorious, high-profile methods possible. Their radical behaviour can be interpreted as a vehement denial of the old beliefs, which had destroyed countries and societies with unimaginable repercussions.

Interestingly, a former member, who cited danger and proximity as reasons, described the atmosphere of the Baader-Meinhof gang in the late 1960s and early 1970s as 'erotic'. Violence was not necessarily the turn-on, but more likely the adrenaline rush, the thrill of adventure that sets the heart racing.

Alongside this political upheaval in Europe and America, women were openly rebelling against the constricting social elements that denied them equality with men. One of the most symbolic acts of this era was the 1968 bra-burning demonstration. Not only was this a statement against the last remaining constricting garment, but it was also a calculated move for women to set themselves apart from previous generations. Bare breasts under thin sweaters and tunics did not signal a woman's availability but a new control over her own body and sexuality. The age of the 'tease' was over and virginity no longer carried the same currency. Women abandoned sexual passivity and embraced the opportunity to sexually express themselves without caring about the outdated moral values of their parents' generation.

As women rejected the domestic roles that had chained them for years, the image of femininity underwent a huge transformation. A necessarily aggressive process, it meant that the

Above: The unforgettable sex bomb, Sophia Loren.

Right: Sex kitten, Brigitte Bardot.

female body had to be de-emphasized for a while in order for women to be taken seriously. Feminists of the 1970s pronounced lingerie taboo, as something that turned women into sex objects. Emphasizing breasts or legs was considered 'unsisterly' because it signalled that the woman wanted to be seduced by a man.

PUNK AND SEX

Culturally, the 1970s were incredibly important in shaping the attitudes that we take for granted some 20 years later. It was an era of confusion and reaction to the previous two decades, an era where glamour and romanticism shared space with confrontational punk expressions. This period was the true beginning of the diversity that characterizes the 1990s. The values embraced by youth culture had their roots in glamour, heroism and an aggressive sexuality. In the last attempt of its kind in contemporary history, music created the basis of an anarchic attitude that refused to believe in the hypocrisies of the past. It was essentially in the 1970s that England saw many of the long-standing social taboos broken down.

Leading the way were shops like Vivienne Westwood and Malcom McLaren's 'SEX' on the King's Road. Sex shops in Soho at that time were called names like 'Tunnel of Love' or 'Temple of Venus': that was about the most explicit that the British sensibility could handle. Westwood and McLaren ensured that they countered this prudish inclination by displaying the name of their shop in six-foot-high pink vinyl letters. The shop was used almost as an art installation, a canvas to deliver out-of-the-ordinary ideas directly to the people. What Westwood and McLaren basically did was to publicize their beliefs through their commercial outlet, and so, by association, did their customers.

Translated for the 1990s, Agent Provocateur embodies the same philosophy. Dissenters relegate the Soho shop as just a 'place to buy knickers', but that, of course, is merely the starting point. The shop is a forum for ideas and beliefs that counteract the apathy of an over-exposed society. Consider the window displays: 'Boycott Shell' stickers stuck all over a naked model, for example, may have nothing specifically to do with lingerie, but everything to do with important reasons for choosing to align yourself with certain merchandise. This may seem like a digression, but the motivations behind our shop lie specifically in the conscious decision to make a statement that has nothing to do with market trends or clever ways to sell a product. In an age and environment in which we seem to be inundated with choice, but are really being offered much the same thing with different marketing policies, it is somewhat anarchic to offer true choice. If marketing is about grouping people together in an anti-individual way, then the opposite of this must be to appeal on a personal level by saying, 'We are like you; you are like us'. This is the attitude at the heart of Agent Provocateur – the kindling of the fire by recognition – an invitation to allow us to fuel the desire, almost like a lover.

'The desirable does not gratify my desire, but deepens it, feeding me, as it were, with fresh hungers.'

Emmanuel Lévinas

Left: An early publicity shot for SEX. Vivienne, Chrissy and Jordon spell it out.

POWER AND CONFUSION

During the 1970s, one of those at the forefront of the changing representation of the feminine erotic was the photographer Helmut Newton. He combined 'nudes' with exactly the kind of fetishistic props that had made the earlier illustrations of Stanton and Willie so notorious. Newton's women lack innocence, but they are beautiful and breathtakingly erotic. They are formidable; they possess, command and inspire strength. His images are credited with a timeless quality that is at the heart of the feminine mystique, as they 'transcend the present and its impermanence' (Noemi Smolik). Incorporating the leitmotifs of pure fetishism – high heels, stockings, lingerie – which create an atmosphere of sexual tension, Newton portrays the erotic figure of women at its most powerful.

It is possible to question whether Newton actually likes women. Using a detailed, specific eroticism, his photographs depict a world that is dominated by women, but of what kind? They are patrician and Olympian, the Fascist ideal of purity. The kind of arousal his photographs elicit has perhaps more to do with the exciting unreality of these objectified, perfected female forms than with their relation to living, breathing women. He gives us sex as power, but really forces you to search for the tenderness or softness that complete the ideal of femininity.

There is an electric energy that surrounds his figures. If it were possible to open a magic door and enter the world of his pictures, you feel that if you dared to touch, you would immediately be struck down by lightning. Perhaps Newton's vision is most exciting because he touches on that which appeals about femininity; one never knows who is in control. The excitement of that mystery is at the heart of his genius.

Right: Helmut Newton's **A Study in Voyeurism**, Paris, 1975.

Though the 1960s and 1970s are characterized
by mass movements that instigated social change,
underneath these historical events people were, of
course, still living their lives. Rather than women
appearing as victims of their circumstances, by being chained to the political ideas of feminism or domestic
roles, Newton's pictures, along with those of Raquel Welch or James Bond girls in tiny bikinis, illustrated a
new freedom to female sexuality.

The true legacy of the 1970s is the ultimate acceptance by society of any confrontational expression
or the manipulation of anything that is shocking for its 'shock value'. In music or fashion, for
example, the shocking becomes the norm. Ideas that seemed controversial were turned
into mere marketing ploys because they grabbed the imagination. Suddenly sex was out
in the open, and everyone was interested in it as a commodity like any other. This
created a culture that, through its rejection of the past, became 'anti-ideas'. Punk rock
culture simply did not have enough substance to sustain it as an interesting idea on a
permanent level. Punk was about the destruction of the past by a generation that
rejected all conformity to any established system and, instead, wanted to smash it
up. The change that occurred in the 1970s was about clearing space to make way
for new ideas, rather than the creation of new ideas.

The breakdown of taboos and rejection of 'right-on' ideals left society in a new
confusion. Barriers had been demolished, but no one knew what they wanted,
resulting in a kind of fragmentation where greed and ostentation became acceptable.
The explicitly feminine image was further sidelined as the underlying social
attitude moved away from high ideals and became totally self-centred. As
women adopted the visual trappings of masculinity in order to succeed
professionally, femininity was celebrated through female earning
power rather than the female body. Power-dressing was a kind
of necessary cross-dressing, which downplayed all the things
that were uniquely female, like high heels and lingerie.

The female icon of the 1980s was the power woman, as epitomized by
Margaret Thatcher. The fetishistic potential of Thatcher's image is enormous –
she is the perfect suburban-England dominatrix. One can easily imagine her on
her day off in cheap six-inch stilettos holding a whip with a submissive 'suit'
cowering at her feet, and of course the ubiquitous handbag somewhere in the
background. This fantasy simply illustrates the invincible nature of the erotic
feminine image. She is perhaps the antithesis of an arousing woman, but
nevertheless, a definite sexual element manifests itself – if you can bring
yourself to picture it!

That women would rise to heights of corporate, academic and artistic success was inevitable. Women were no longer objects of seduction but powerful and provocative seducers, as well as highly competent professionals. With the power of equality, and with the right and ability to choose, there was a yearning to return to an expression of femininity that had been put aside in order to succeed. It was time for a return to femininity by exploiting female charms, and what better way to draw attention to female power than by emphasizing the feminine form?

AGENT PROVOCATEUR

Like the small spark that starts an inferno, we triggered a change in attitude with the opening of our first shop in 1994. These are eclectic times, especially in terms of the roles of women and what they wear to fulfil those roles. If there is one belief that is rarely spoken about in connection with Agent Provocateur, it is the belief in the absolute and fascinating uniqueness of the feminine. We recreated the look of the pin-up girl for the 1990s as one which does not represent female subjugation. She is a woman who can think for herself, make choices and is in control.

We celebrate many aspects of the feminine – beauty, arousal, strength, honesty and knowledge – and use these qualities to design concept-based lingerie that literally creates an agent provocateur out of the woman who wears it. Our lingerie appeals not only to a physical manifestation of sexuality, the visually erotic, but also to that part of the intellect that is most deeply excited and stimulated by such images and sensations. Our lingerie is a reaction against mass media and the lager culture of cheap thrills. It is special, it takes time, it is secret and personal – it is a dedication to make the utmost of your sexual expression on a day-to-day basis. We have been responsible for placing lingerie fairly and squarely on the fashion map, and the interest aroused can be seen repeated in all the major fashion brands from the high street to Bond Street. The phenomenon was really a result of women's response to the lingerie. Finally, here was a company that was not trying to bore women into selection, but actively encouraged excitement and seduction – a company as individual as themselves. Most importantly, a company that wanted women to be as female as possible, as utterly different from men: fantastically, explicitly, feminine. By no means do we advocate a return to the 1950s, but simply espouse a philosophy that takes the equal rights of women as a given, while believing women can, and indeed should, still look as sexy and feminine as possible.

43

Opposite: Kina's tied up right now and can't come to the phone.

Left: Meanwhile... Natasha looks for a man.

A woman came into the Broadwick Street shop with some underwear that had been given to her. 'I can't possibly wear this,' she said. Thinking that the lingerie was in some way faulty, we asked why. 'Because,' she replied, 'I'm a feminist.' This woman was basically saying that to be a feminist you could not look feminine. She perfectly illustrates the confusion some people are in. We believe that the ultimate expression is for each individual woman to emphasize her femininity and to revel in her erotic life. After all, the instinct to display and attract is inescapable. The desire to be sexy and the innate sexiness of the body remain, no matter how it is politicized. If you've got it, flaunt it. If you don't have it,

get some!

Chapter 2   The Body

As this is about the body, let us start with the brain.

'The taste for coloured underwear has been analysed as a blatant expression of the erotic impulse.'

Amy De La Haye, ed., THE CUTTING EDGE

Why is lingerie sexy? Serious lingerie requires thought, time and effort. That is, thought, time and effort put into looking and feeling arousing, sexy, special. Lingerie's intimacy with the body is what primarily makes it so exciting - it literally touches our most private places. In some ways, lingerie acts as a withholding; a holding back of the body while increasing the sense of mystery that surrounds it. Lingerie can be an alternative to the naked body, with certain fabrics exciting different sensations, or it can be an exquisite wrapping of the offered 'gift'. Lingerie lifts the naked body out of the ordinary or, better still, the 'natural', and presents the body as something supernatural, extraordinary - a glorification of nature.

CORSETS

The bodice was stoutly whaleboned, long and ridged, something from the days when wasp-waists were in fashion, and was fitted with gussets upon which the breasts lay. The tighter it was drawn, the more prominently O's breasts rose, pushed up by the supporting gussets, and the more sharply upward her nipples were tilted. At the same time her waist was constricted, her womb and buttocks were made to swell out. The odd thing is that this veritable cuirass was exceedingly comfortable and, up to a certain point, relaxing. In it, one felt very upright, but, without one being able to tell how or why unless it was by contrast, it increased one's consciousness of the freedom, or rather the availability, of the parts it left unencompassed.

Pauline Réage, THE STORY OF O

The corset, perhaps, has the most interesting story in the history of lingerie - an instrument of torture or an erotic device? At the end of the century, this is largely a matter of opinion. One thing is certain: in terms of emphasizing the female form, of exaggerating femininity, the corset still reigns supreme. However functional the corset may have been initially, its restrictive and deforming side effects remain firmly fixed in the past. This complex and provocative garment first became popular after the Renaissance in the wake of the most severe Catholicism that spread throughout Europe from Spain. For the next 300 years the corset asserted its domination over the female form, with a brief respite during the years of the French Revolution. As a symbol of the aristocracy, the corset was then rejected, but

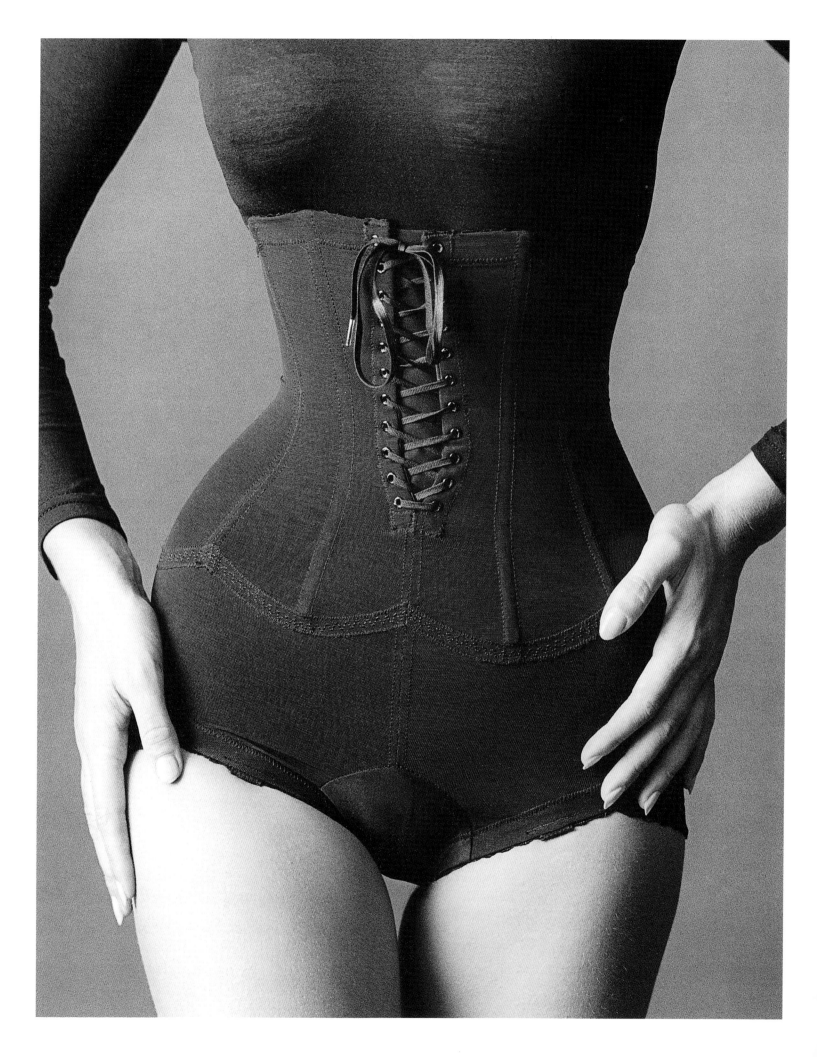

the image the hourglass silhouette was too deeply embedded in the Western psyche, and at the beginning of the 1800s, the corset was once again at the forefront of fashion.

> The woman of the 1840s, in her corset and crinolines, appeared spectacularly useless. The less natural her appearance, the more seductive she became. Her body was hidden under a great quantity of fabric trimmed with ribbons and frills. Laced, fastened and buttoned into the complexities of her dress, she simultaneously offered and withheld herself.
>
> Beatrice Fontanel, Support and Seduction

The corset has always been a garment with erotic connotations. In 1876 the painter Édouard Manet declared that 'the satin corset is perhaps the nude of our time'. It is impossible to say what the most appealing thing is about the corset. Is it the arched back or the slim waist? Is it the whole silhouette or simply the effect of lifting the breasts? An observer might say it is the thrill of knowing that the softness of the female body is encased or stoppered like a shaken bottle of champagne, while the wearer might enjoy the sensation of support, almost like being held very tightly. Perhaps it is the knowledge of how ultimately feminine, and subsequently how ultimately powerful a woman looks when so defined. Perhaps we are moved, as we are by art or sculpture, to elevate the hourglass figure as something to be admired or revered – which is the practice of the fetishist. It might be the anticipation of the lacing and unlacing, the slow revealing of flesh, or inversely the sensation of satin, lace or leather against skin that is naturally naked. Inside the corset, the female body is strenuously guarded by a complicated system of hooks and laces, and therefore becomes that which is forbidden. What is perhaps most exciting is that while the corset guards the body, it also suggests the wearer has a calculated interest in the sensations of sex and in erotic life.

51

Left: Tighter!...Tighter! John Willie, master of Bizarre.

VOL 1 No. 4   1946

BIZARRE

THIRTY-FIVE CENTS

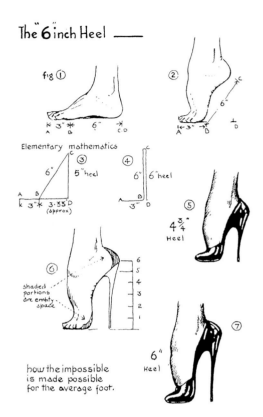

The "6" inch Heel ——

fig ① ... ②

Elementary mathematics ③ ... ④

⑤ 4¾" Heel

⑥ shaded portions are empty space

how the impossible is made possible for the average foot.

⑦ 6" Heel

52

WHAT ABOUT HIGH HEELS?

No item of lingerie has been as objectified as the high heel. Are high heels lingerie?

Perhaps not in the strictest sense, however no erotic image of a beautifully undressed woman is complete without a heel of at least five inches. Different reasons have been given, of course, such as the leg is lengthened, the body is streamlined so the feet are no longer at right angles but create 'a graceful taper, fading away to nothing' (John Willie, Bizarre).

What is most tempting? The arch of the instep, reminiscent of the back arched in pleasure, or the bum slightly raised to be caressed, or ... Perhaps it is the steps of a woman in very high heels, the absolute antithesis of the masculine stride, or the way the skirt rides up ever so slightly when a woman walks up the stairs in heels. They are fuck-me-IF-you-can-catch-me shoes, giving pleasure through the knowledge of the effect they are having on you, the powerless voyeur.

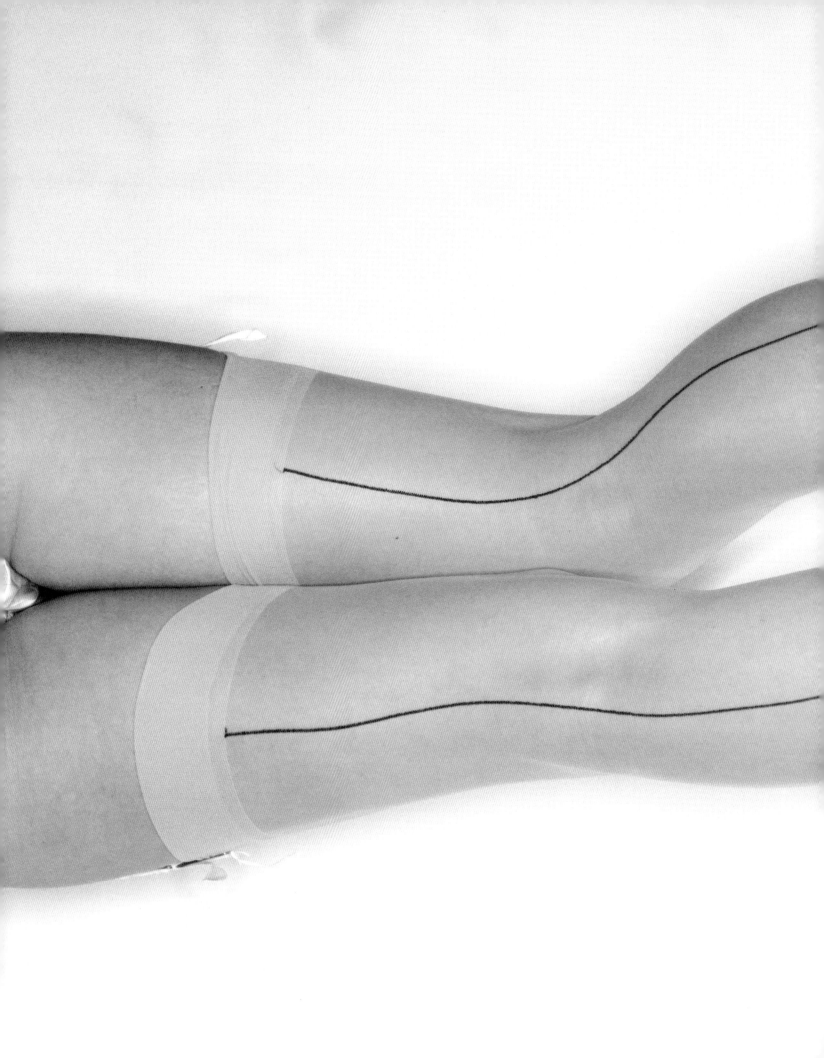

'Whenever I
interview a
model I first
inspect her legs
– from the tip of
her toes to the
top of her hose.'

ELMER BATTERS

STOCKINGS AND SUPENDERS

Some of us believe that suspender belts are the
prerogative of a superior kind of woman, bold enough to
exploit all her assets - the 'feminine' woman who has
made the notion of 'women as sex object' obsolete.

Giles Néret, 1000 Dessous

The most enduring impression of the suspender is that
of a frame for a priceless and unique creation; the curve of the
fabric over the top of the hips leads down to the top of the
stockings. Imagine tulle suspenders in a delicate turquoise, no
knickers, focusing attention on the centre of pleasure.

What about the sensation of wearing them? Suspenders
rubbing gently against the thighs, naughtily pressing together the
bare tops of the legs under a skirt while no one else knows what
you are doing.

The intricacy of suspenders; the placement of the belt
around the waist must always be just so, while the attachment
of the stocking is a delicate procedure that requires concentration,
so the stocking not only remains in place but does not drag the belt
down when you walk. Now, the posture adopted for the fastening
of stockings - fantastic!

Stockings create lines. What does the seam invite the hand, the eye,
to do? To slowly follow the seam up from the ankle to the gap of hidden
flesh at the top of the leg. This tiny warm space of flesh, exposed
between stocking top and the line of the knicker is one of the most
erotic images and touch sensations. Fishnets, like veils, tantalize
with their flashes of skin. The associations of fishnets with
showgirls and starlets adds an extra frisson in the 1990s,
glamorous and out of the ordinary.

Left: Refreshing the
parts other beers
cannot reach.

Above: The ultimate goal – the warm gap of flesh between silky stockings and taut suspenders.

Right: Showing off her stockings as only Betty Page knows how.

Opposite: Framed from behind at the Café de Paris.

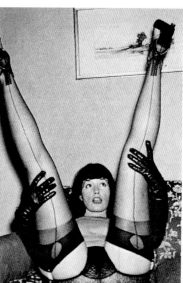

KNICKERS | Where does a girl keep her diary or her love letters? Where can she hide all those naughty things that are the props for her secret life? In her knicker drawer of course! There is something deliciously wicked about looking in a girl's knicker drawer and accessing the most intimate of all garments. Imagine her in white cotton when she is in a schoolgirl mood, or pink leopard-print for an outrageous attitude. Serious fun begins with the tying of the ribbons either side of a black shiny brief, while scraps of silk in the bright touch-me-feel-me colours of deep red, purple and fuchsia are everyday favourites, a private boost to her working day. The sheer tulles and nets are strictly to be shown off - from any angle. Right at the back, wrapped in tissue paper, is Friday night's surprise: delicate black lace, edged with mint-green ribbon and discreetly split from front to back.

60

Right: Tie-side knickers are the best for stripping.

Opposite: This way up - Rachel Williams in Agent Provocateur tulle knickers.

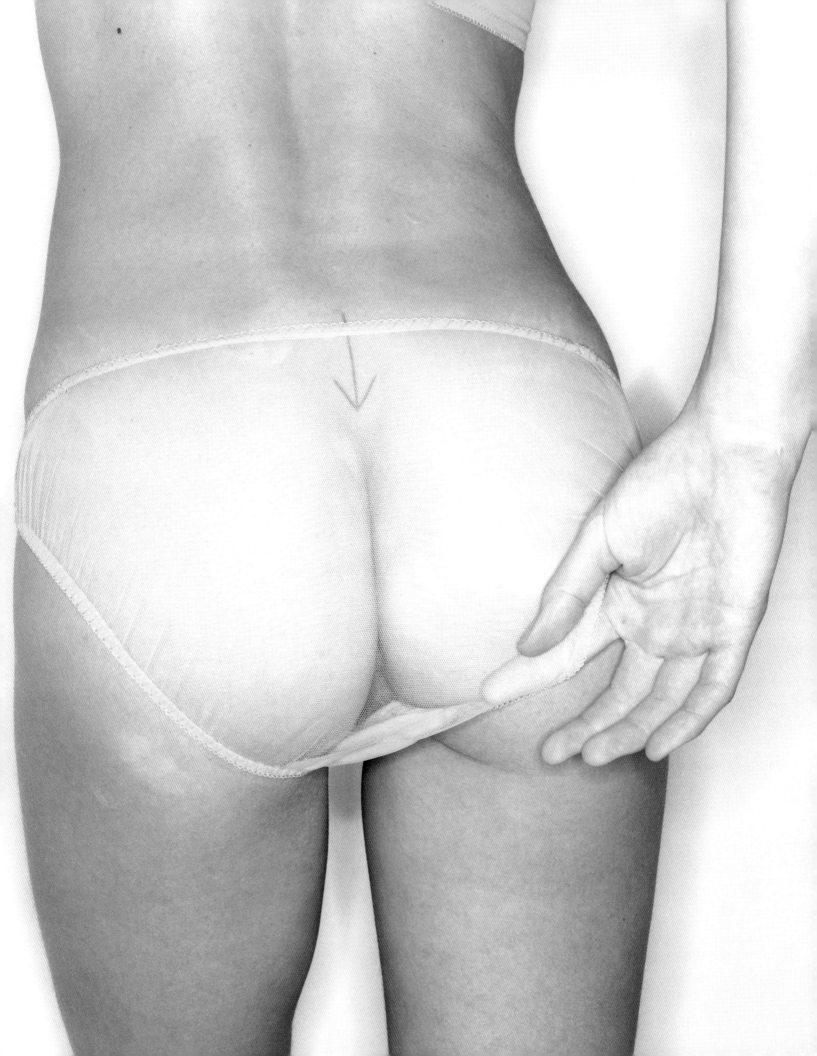

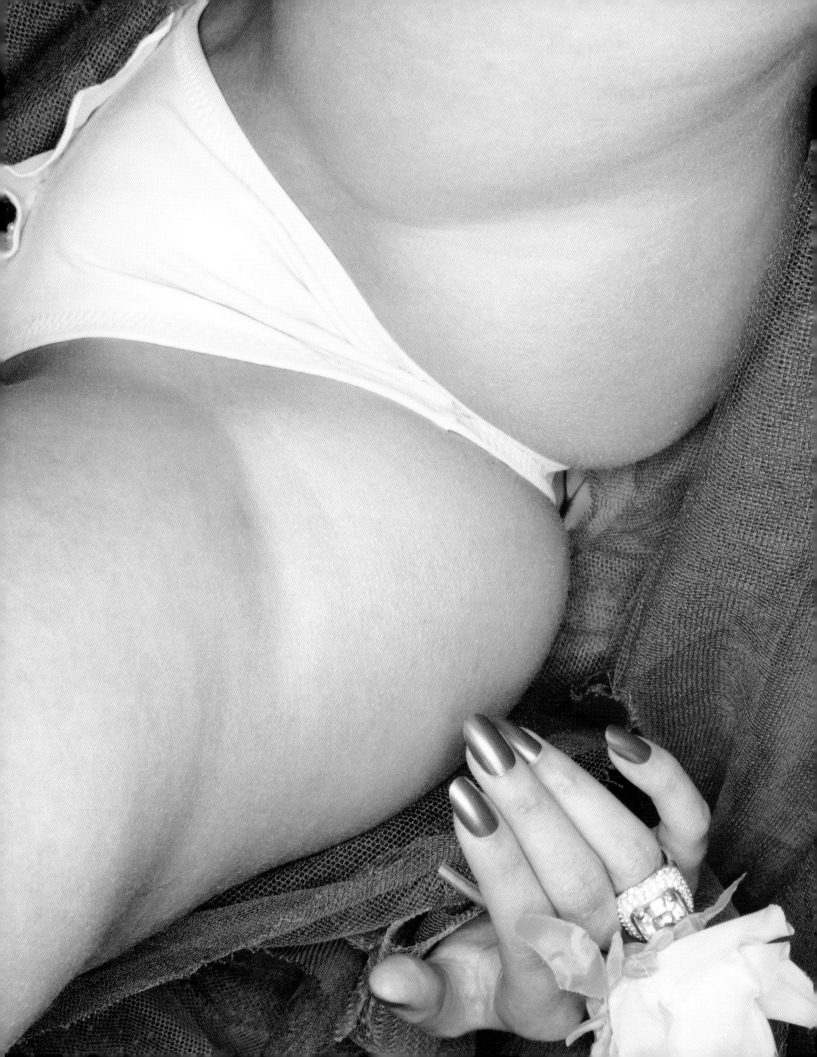

BRASSIERE | Although the main function of the bra is, and has always been, support, this is by no means the only thing that a bra can do. Perhaps the most tantalizing piece of modern lingerie, the bra shapes a woman's breasts, giving a different look with each shape. What could be more erotic or more feminine than the curve of the breasts supported in a piece of fine lingerie that perfectly complements them? Push-up, balcony, bras that separate, those which squeeze together, water bras, half cups, soft cups, stretch fit – the options are endless and it

all depends on what and how you want to show off. True temptation comes with something daring. The quarter cup gently lifts the breasts and cuts across the nipples, squeezing together, pushing, exerting just the slightest pressure, while brightly coloured tulle wraps the breasts like sweet candy. Straps that are meant to be seen should have a little bow where they join the cup, showing that they support something special, while shocking-pink lace teases the eye under shirts that gape oh so slightly.

'As a Playboy Bunny and Playmate of the Year, I recognize the true celebration of women and sex. For me, Agent Provocateur defines both beautifully. As an agent on a mission, I always feel that frisson of excitement on just entering Agent Provocateur. Because it is the headquarters for our planned conspiracies, it is where we must go for equipment to incite desire and inflict pleasure on our selected targets, the men we intend to torment and delight, or where we go, as Emily Dickinson once put it, simply to "dwell in possibility". Wherever our targets lead us, whether it's an elevator in the World Trade Center, a card table in a Vegas casino or a quiet corner of the Scientology Center, remember with Agent Provocateur, any assignment is possible.'

Marilyn Cole Lownes

BOUDOIR | The boudoir is the most intimate of rooms, a space for indulging and pampering. This is the perfect place to be glamorous and naughty, privately, while no one is looking. Enter the world of a woman: lit, scented, and scattered with clothes, books and secret treasures. It is here that she takes off her working-day clothes and slips into 'something a little more comfortable' that requires no hooks or buttons or fastenings. There is nothing as indulgent as dressing up to stay in the bedroom, turning your own space into the most entrancing of locations. There is an air of sweet nostalgia about the long peignoir with marabou trim that covers a bias-cut gown in almost transparent silk. Recall an era of lost allure with feet slipped into delicate marabou slippers with satin heels, perfect for practising elegantly seductive poses. Short flirty babydolls can cause trouble, looking as they do so naughty yet so innocent. The favourite of the Exotic Girls of the 1950s, the babydoll is the perfect outfit for mixing martinis and playing the temptress. Sometimes it pays to be serious though, and a serious mood requires a seriously sexy garment that clings and only just conceals, allowing the outlines of curves, the glow of skin, to be faintly seen. Each complements a woman's body perfectly. The lingerie lies, draped over chaises and chairs, discarded as she explores; colours, styles and fabrics open up new personas and possibilities.

'The young men liked to visit Mathilde. She turned her shop into a boudoir, full of chaises-longues, lace and satin, curtains and pillows…

'When they arrived, it was scented with burning incense. The only light came from illuminated glass globes filled with water and iridescent fish, corals and sea horses. This gave the room an undersea aspect, the appearance of a dream, a place where three beautiful women exhaled such sensual auras that a man would have been overcome.'

Anaïs Nin, DELTA OF VENUS

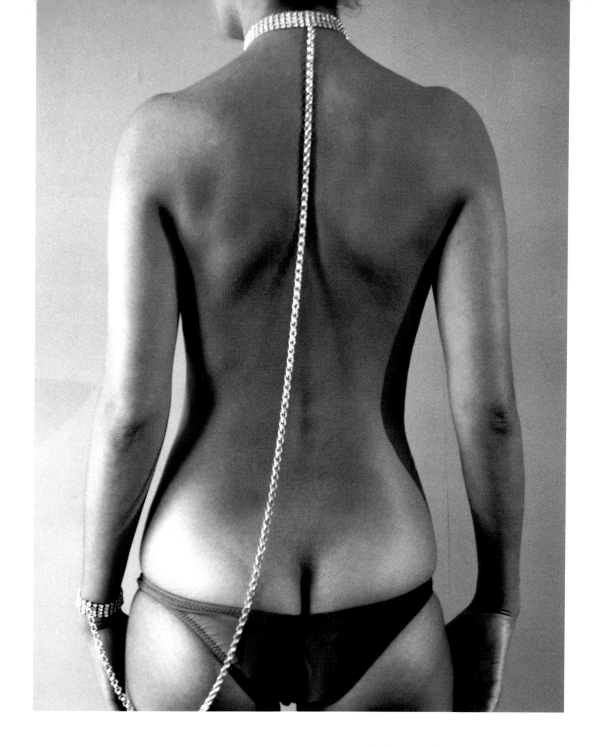

WHIPS, COLLARS AND CUFFS

A whole new dimension is added to the erotic experience with each little accessory that adorns the naked body. Showgirl fantasies would not be complete without sequinned nipple tassels and a sparkling choker that mesmerize as they move. Heavy diamanté cuffs add a hint of subtle fetishism to a party outfit. Sophisticated domination games are played out by the excitement of ideas. A hand holding a beautiful crystal-handled whip, or a neck encircled by a delicate silver collar and lead, lends a delightful thrill of fear to an evening's entertainment. Theatricals can extend long into the night as sex kittens pout in pussycat collars and exotic Arabian bellydancers remove seven veils to reveal glittering anklets and bellychains. This is the realm of adventure - a personal journey into the dark, the exotic and the sensual world.

Chapter 3

Design & CONSTRUCTION

'I think, at the end of the day, there's a certain kind of woman who likes to

dress for sex. . .

they want to do it properly and they want to do it right, and I want them to do it properly and right too!' Joseph Corré, **TV Interview**

When we first started Agent Provocateur, we had no intention of becoming designers. We had a concept about creating an environment that was erotic, intimate and luxurious, that had a sense of fashion, adventure, comfort, colour and glamour along with an element of fantasy; a place where people would feel comfortable enough to indulge in their erotic side. This idea created a special kind of frame, and all we had to do was to find products that we liked to fill it. This proved more difficult than we thought; our assumption that the world must be full of these delightful little things was totally wrong. We found an abundance of fairly basic-looking, functional underwear, without a hint of any of the qualities associated with fashion, glamour or fantasy. At the opposite end of the scale were cheap, slightly ludicrous, sex-shop garments, which appealed to the British 'Carry-On' mentality and perpetuated the idea that underwear should be cheap and cheerful, whether it was basic white knickers or badly-fitted PVC pants.

Although we were moderately successful in finding some items, mostly French, that suited our taste, we were able to fill the gap by sourcing original vintage garments from the 1950s and 1960s that reflected the silhouettes we wanted to promote. These garments, through their construction and attention to detail, were a source of inspiration to us. Even though they were more than 40 years old, they had a real sense of creativity about them. Not only that, but the fit was incredible; they really worked, and put any other contemporary figure-forming lingerie to shame.

We searched high and low all over the world but found very little else. At that point it became obvious that we would have to start designing and working with manufacturers to make our fantasies reality. However, no one was interested in making small quantities of high-quality garments that really formed the female body because the enterprise was not commercial enough. Most of the manufacturers would not take our concept seriously, and could not believe that we were interested in the pieces we were. For example, if we selected something like an old-fashioned roll-on from their collection, they would look at us like we were mad. They said that no modern woman would wear it, that it was totally unattractive, even though we knew we could do something special with it and transform it into something desirable. Far from wanting to discuss whether our ideas for lingerie were feasible, manufacturers were only interested in how much we would be prepared to pay, whereas we wanted to create garments that had a quality about them which suggested every decision had been thought about, whatever the cost.

THE CRAFT

The craft of supporting and displaying the female body is not one that can be taught, like the making of a fine shirt. The intensely personal nature of lingerie-making ensures that each person with an original vision of how to envelop breasts and buttocks must start from scratch, without pattern or guide.

Any design discipline might be used in the construction of a bra. For example, the entrepreneur, film-maker and aeroplane enthusiast Howard Hughes famously designed Jane Russell's aerodynamic 'Cantilever' bra for his film, THE OUTLAW, after the costume mistress insisted that she was a designer, not an architect. In fact, from a technical point of view, coming from a fashion background did not make things any easier. The transition from making clothes, which come in four or five sizes, to making our bras, which come in a minimum of 12, sometimes up to 18 different sizes, was a complete culture shock, especially since the difference in size can be just half an inch.

Anything that has to fit the bust is incredibly complicated to get right. Even before assembling the garment, the right balance has to be found between the fabric, interliners, underwires, adjusters, trimmings, lace, fastenings and elastics, and even this can only be perfected initially through trial and error. For example, each tiny adjustment to the fabric means that the quality and type of the other components will also have to be altered.

Almost unbelievably, and as recently as 1958, detailed manuals were available, such as the one by a 'Mademoiselle Etienne', showing how women at home could make their own bras, corsets and girdles. Corsets themselves are now a specialized craft, and finding anyone who still makes corsets in the traditional way is difficult. The corset was the mainstay of fashion for centuries before the First World War.

It defined whatever was the fashionable shape of the moment and, more often than not, was horribly constricting, contorting the body into exaggerated shapes to achieve the desired silhouette. Modern corsets are rarely worn for practical reasons, but more for accentuating the female form. Although they have a strong erotic image, they need to have the comfort modern women expect from their clothes. They are certainly meant to be shown off. They must be beautiful and, for us, beautifully made. Even though crinolines are no longer the fashion of the day, corsets are still one of the most versatile garments because they retain their original spirit – a woman can still build her outfit around the one she is wearing. The modern corset looks most like the corsets of the late 1800s, though the roots of their manufacture are from the 1950s, the last time when such foundation garments were regularly worn.

Corsets are based around an interliner of stiff fabric, such as broch, which is lined for comfort. The bones are made of flattened metal spirals so that they are durable but flexible enough not to snap when the wearer sits down. The front of the corset is joined by a two-piece metal busc with fastenings. In the back, either side of the eyelets, are the nuly bones, which are stronger than the metal spirals, support the back and hold the lacing in place. The corset is then covered in fabric and any kind can be used, such as silk, satin, lace or even leather. A finely-made corset will be finished by hand. If it is made entirely by hand it can take an experienced corsetier up to two days to complete. Even so, a corset requires many machines for all the various operations, such as a straight stitcher, a zigzagger, a binder, an eyelet machine and a tool to punch holes. Most off-the-peg corsets will only go up to a 30-inch waist, but you can get one specially made in any size. When buying a corset, choose a size smaller than your actual waist size in order for it to fit properly.

DESIGN, COLOUR AND FABRIC

Inspiration comes in many forms. When designing lingerie that is meant to be sexually appealing, and which might be revealed to the person of the wearer's choice, you must keep this situation in mind. You must imagine the girl undressing in front of her lover or in front of her mirror and how it will make her feel, because it should excite, create a feeling of something special, like a wedding dress or an evening gown. One of the most important ways of doing this is by using colour. We feel that we have been instrumental in the introduction of luxury combined with colour, rather than coloured lingerie being kinky or simply seasonal. Half the excitement lies in showing off a glimpse of colour under a serious suit, letting a chosen person know there is something different about you, something vibrant and alive.

Initial inspiration can come from many different sources; however, most of the time, it comes from looking at the past and realizing what can be achieved by translating those ideas using new fabrics. In other instances inspiration can come purely from the fabric itself – there is nothing like the thrill of stumbling across an unusual fabric that feeds the imagination and turns a classic garment, like a corset, into something completely modern. We do have a tendency to look to the past for our inspiration because people really were more creative with the limited choices they had and they experimented with fabrics. The fabric is of prime importance. Not only does it have to be practical, but it also must look beautiful and feel sensual, pleasurable, to the wearer. One of the most erotic fabrics is lace because of its transparent, intricately patterned look. Lace has always been used for lingerie and has that special, luxurious feeling, but it is a notoriously difficult material with which to work because it is so fine and delicate. Silk satin or crêpe de chine create a feeling of luxury, while sheer tulle is definitely for a sexy sensation. All of these are traditional fabrics but are not used much by larger manufacturers because of the misconception that a stretch fabric will be more comfortable and fit more women.

However, if the bra or the knickers are well made and thought out, they will fit perfectly and be extremely comfortable. The fabrics used for making bras, in particular, have varied greatly. During and after the Second World War, the industry used discarded parachute silk, and the elastic panel in the first 'sports corset' was made by Dunlop!

We are always experimenting with new, unusual fabrics. Even if they do not ultimately work, that does not stop us from trying. Advances in technology have meant that mass volumes of styles are possible, but they just do not have the feel of something into which a lot of imagination has gone. Sometimes the

Waisted
Effort

Elvgren

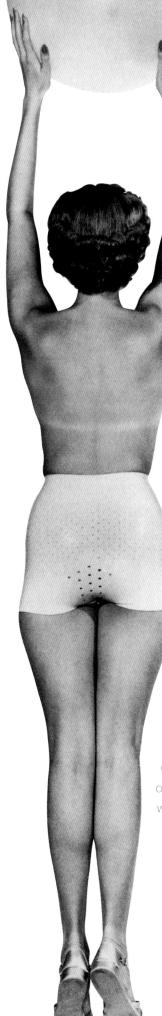

fabric quality or fit is compromised for the sake of putting the required number of products on the shelves, and that this has come to be accepted as the norm is terrible. The whole process of corsetry is organic, in that it has a natural growth or development, like a living thing. As with growing a garden, it takes time and dedication, and can be frustrating, but the end result is beautiful and worth waiting for.

MALE AND FEMALE PERSPECTIVES

Although lingerie is designed for women, the male perspective is really important. The best, most desirable, result can only be achieved through the balance of both male and female perspectives. Lingerie really has to be an equally pleasurable and stimulating experience for both partners, because such beautiful underwear is designed to be shown off one way or another.

When looking at a prototype or a new range for the first time, we consider primarily whether the garment fits the purpose and whether it does the job it is supposed to do in terms of support and fit. The immediate visual impact should be alluring and sexually appealing. This is the point where the male and female perspective comes into play. We consider how the lingerie looks on the body from both perspectives of what is erotic, and we question the models as to how the lingerie feels to wear. The female viewpoint is more subtle than the male – more concerned with what a woman likes or dislikes about her body, which is often different from what her boyfriend might think. In some ways, a woman's idea of what is sexy is far more intricate than what the man thinks is sexy, and that is the problem when men buy underwear for their girlfriends. Men may buy lingerie for their fantasy woman, who may be quite different from their girlfriend. Women love to show off and display themselves, but it has to be on their own terms. A woman does not want to be on show as someone else's fantasy girl. It absolutely has to correspond with her idea of what is sexy as well, and obviously, in the end, this makes for a much more satisfying experience.

When we combine our ideas and perspectives, then the lingerie appeals to both sexes, but on the rare occasions that we don't, it will usually appeal to one or the other sex. When we design, we think about all shapes, sizes and types of women. Sometimes we will have a really good idea for lingerie or a bikini that will only appeal to a certain shape of woman, but we will go ahead with it anyway, because what we always aim for, and what we like to believe, is that there is something at Agent Provocateur for everyone.

Left: An original Playtex rubber girdle, which went on sale in 1945. It had special holes in the gusset for ventilation.

Chapter 4

Fashion

Vivienne Westwood,   PAINTED LADIES, BBC TV

It is impossible to appreciate clothing of any period without an understanding of what goes on underneath it. While historically women relied on foundation garments to give them the figure that fashion dictated, more recently underwear is about luxury and pleasure as much as about fashion or form. As to the question of which came first - foundation or fashion - it is hard to say. When you think of the particular 'look' of a period, what comes to mind first is the silhouette or shape of the female figure, as opposed to the details of the dress. As well as a brief history of foundation, this chapter looks at how other undergarments became fashionable and eroticized, for fashion is, and always has been, about looking and feeling attractive.

THE BODICE

Strangely enough, the first bodice for women was directly influenced by men's fashion, in particular the pourpoint jacket, which was worn to protect the body from the metal armour that had replaced chain mail. The pourpoint revolutionized clothing because, for the first time, fabric was cut to fit the body. The jacket had a separate sleeve piece, enabling greater freedom of movement when wielding arms, and was also heavily padded in the front to follow the lines of armour. The heroic, macho look, combined with the fitted comfort of the jacket, made it an accidental fashion success.

It was not until the beginning of the 1500s that a separate bodice and skirt became fashionable. With this development, the bodice became straighter and tighter, and the skirt fuller. The bodice, the ancestor of all corsets, did not have the side boning of later corsets until the 1550s, but it did have what is known as the 'busc' - a rigid piece of wood, horn, whalebone, ivory or even metal which was inserted down the front of the corset to keep it straight. The busc was often beautifully engraved and could be removed and transferred between corsets. It was tied in place by a busc lace, which ladies would give to their chosen gallant to wear on his arm or hatband as a sign of favour. The Spanish farthingale underskirt was worn with the bodice and created a silhouette that resembled a lady wearing enormous side panniers.

The 1600s saw a lowering of necklines and the rejection of the farthingale. The boned bodice remained, but was shorter, and skirts stayed full by the wearing of petticoats. The emphasis was on the breasts, which were compressed by the bodice to stick up over the top of the dress as if they were trying to escape!

The women of the eighteenth century were, perhaps, the most decorated of any period in time. In response to the puritanism and rigid morals that had prevailed over the end of the previous century, women flaunted an excessively feminine figure, both in the shape and the dazzling decoration of the dress.

The corset was still evolving, however, and the increasing availability of whalebone meant that the ridged busc could be dispensed with in favour of a slightly more flexible, but nevertheless highly structured, boned corset. Gowns of the time succumbed to the craft of the corsetier, and were sometimes worn open at the front, especially Court or formal gowns, which would have also left the shoulders bare. This kind of corset blurred the boundaries between fashion and foundation, for although the corset was most definitely underwear, it was meant to be shown off, as 'the eighteenth-century craftsman never wasted his art' (Norah Waugh, CORSETS AND CRINOLINES).

The skirt that accompanied the corset was the hooped petticoat. The large full crinoline, which created the slender-topped, bell-shaped silhouette, was worn for formal dress only; otherwise, pocket hoops were worn, which extended either side of the waist, with the dress caught up and draped on the sides. A large pad, usually made of cork, was attached to the rear to make the bottom stick out, and this was the precursor of the bustle. While skirt widths increased to greater and greater proportions, their impracticality drove the men of the day to frustration, probably because of the distance the skirt put between them and the object of their desire!

THE CRINOLINE ON TRIAL

January 4, 1710. The Court being prepared for proceedings on the Cause of the Petticoat, I gave orders to bring in a Criminal who was taken up as she went out of the Puppet-Show about Three Nights ago, and was now standing in the Street with a great Concourse of People about her. Word was brought me, that she had endeavour'd Twice or Thrice to come in, but could not do it by reason of her Petticoat, which was too large for the Entrance of my House, though I had ordered both the Folding-Doors to be thrown open for its Reception. Upon this, I desired the Jury of Matrons, who stood at my Right Hand, to inform themselves of her Condition, and know whether there were any private Reasons why she might not make her Appearance separate from her Petticoat. This was managed with great Discretion, and had such an Effect, that upon the Return of the Verdict from Bench of Matrons, I issued out an Order forthwith That the Criminal should be stripped of her Incumberances, till she become little enough to enter my house.

Norah Waugh, CORSETS AND CRINOLINES, THE TATLER

Left: Fragonard's delightful vision of love in **THE SWING**, 1767, shows the unfolding drama of sexual attraction as the lady displays the secrets that lie under her skirt to her lover.

Following this very public outcry against skirt widths, the gentleman proceeds to put the crinoline on trial, deciding that he 'neither can, nor will allow it'.

GARTERS AND NO KNICKERS

During the 1700s, knickers were unheard of, the linen chemise being considered perfectly adequate. In his **MEMOIRS**, 1855, Lord Cowley recounts:

> Despatch from our Ambassador in Paris on the visit of King Victor Emmanuel. Lord Cowdrey reports that at a state reception a Lady in Waiting had the misfortune to trip over her crinoline skirt and tumble headlong in view of the Imperial party, whereupon the King exclaimed with enthusiasm to the Empress: 'I am delighted to see, Madam, that your ladies do not wear les caleçons, and that the Gates of Paradise are always open!'

Rosemary Hawthorne, KNICKERS: AN INTIMATE APPRAISAL

The device for holding up the stockings - the garter - was considered more erotic than the corset. Made of silk or lengths of ribbon, garters were the gateway to sensual pleasure, the last bastion of clothing before warm, bare flesh. Lovers would be sure of conquest if they got as far as the garter, and for a woman to tie her garters in public, or even show them, was considered highly provocative.

It is not surprising that swinging was such a popular pastime in the 1700s, as Jean Honoré Fragonard's delightful painting THE SWING illustrates. In the foreground, the man lying on the grass has placed himself in the best position to view the treasures of his knicker-less lady.

ILLUSIONS OF NUDITY

Events after the French Revolution also brought dramatic changes in fashion. The silhouette of massive skirts and a projected bottom went out of style as waists moved higher and such fabrics as printed cottons and muslins took over from heavy silks. The figure-hugging dress of the early 1800s dispensed with the need for a corset, and the image of the Greek goddess reigned supreme. The neoclassical period found women emulating nudity in fashion - popular legend has it that women would wet their muslin gowns to make them hang in the style of Greek sculpture. The most popular corsets gave the illusion of nudity. An example of this can be seen in the famous painting by Jacques-Louis David of the celebrated Mme Récamier, reclining on a chaise longue in her chemise. Her breasts are painted far apart, as if separated by a corset, though the chemise was a garment worn under a corset.

In fact, the chemise is a most interesting article of undress, and perhaps one of the first to cross over into fashion and to be eroticized. In the neoclassical period, the chemise looked enough like the outer clothing of ancient Greece to be legitimately portrayed in painting, yet it was actually the most intimate of a woman's garments, worn as it was next to the skin. There was always more erotic interest in showing the chemise than, say, the corset, even though the body of the 'nude' always reflected the corseted shape. Subversively, the white of the shift could indicate purity, while at the same time suggesting the eroticism of the naked body.

Dialogue between a Lady and her Male Milliner
- Citizen I am just come to town, pray have the goodness to inform
  me how I must appear to be in the fashion?
- Madam, 'tis done in a moment, in two minutes I shall equip you
  in the first style. Have the goodness to take off that bonnet.
- Well.
- Off [with] that Petticoat.
- There it is.
- Away with those pockets.
- There they go.
- Throw off that handkerchief.
- 'Tis done.
- Away with that corset and sleeves.
- Will that do?
- Yes, madame, you are now in the fashion: 'Tis an easy matter you
  see - to be dressed in fashion you have only to undress!

Norah Waugh, CORSETS AND CRINOLINES, LADY'S MAGAZINE

92

A NEW CRUSH

The vogue for neoclassicism liberated women from the constriction of stays for a short time, but the idea that the body needed to be supported, and perhaps the allure of the accentuated shape, was too deeply entrenched. Corsets reappeared again very quickly, heralding a new relationship between women, underwear and fashion.

> I have seen, with considerable uneasiness, that stiff stays have been creeping in upon us gradually and almost imperceptibly, till at length, concealment is no longer affected. Tired of being at ease, and ambitious of the sufferings and martyrdom of their grandmothers, our young ladies fearlessly advance to the torture of steel and whalebone, and willingly sacrifice their comfort and wellbeing on what they conceive to be the shrine of elegance and taste.
>
> Norah Waugh, CORSETS AND CRINOLINES, ACKERMANN'S REPOSITORY OF ARTS

More than ever, the emphasis was on curves flowing out from a small waist, and the hourglass silhouette came back with a vengeance. The Second Empire corset, circa 1850-1860, created an unbelievably tiny waist to set off the width of the crinoline, which had also made a comeback. The nineteenth century saw much progress in the evolution of the corset, with the introduction of metal eyelets, two-part buscs that hooked in front, and elasticized lacing, allowing a woman to dress or undress unaided. Apparently, this was a great convenience to women carrying on amorous affairs, as a husband would no longer come back in the evening to find the corset knotted differently to how he tied it that morning!

To the Slaves of Fashion

You must try and lace me tighter, lace me tighter, mother dear;
My waist, you know, is nearly half the size it was last year;
I will not faint again, mother, I care not what they say,
Oh! It's sixteen inches today, mother, it's sixteen inches today.

ENGLISH WOMEN'S DOMESTIC MAGAZINE

93

The corset was to undergo yet another transformation, as women started wearing the bustle around the turn of the century. These were years of the S-bend silhouette, where the corset reached its most complicated, or, as some would say 'its cruel and lunatic extremes' (Beatrice Fontanel, SUPPORT AND SEDUCTION). The corset required to achieve the look was constructed from as many as 10 or 15 pieces per side, with varying quantities of steel and whalebone in different lengths and weights. The imprisoning garment gradually became longer and smoother, coming down well over the thighs, and was laced so tightly that women could not sit down. This was the last time in history that fashion would dictate such a complicated and constricting silhouette.

The early 1900s, called the Belle Époque in France, saw the last of the corset's dominance. Elaborately frilled and ruffled, the corset had a long metal busc that dug into the groin, causing women to arch their backs to give relief and thus create the long, curved silhouette. Absurd, yet elegant, this corset was replaced by a suppler model, which paradoxically freed the ribs from crushing constraint but imprisoned the legs down to the tops of the knees. Nevertheless, Europe was approaching a new era as women's suffrage and the onset of the First World War changed the structure of modern society completely.

WAR AND FREEDOM

The war had a massive impact on women. Not only did they earn the right to vote, but they also took over men's jobs in factories, transport and policing. Contemporary fashion was moving swiftly on to a more emancipated era. The fact that women took more active roles, played sports and rode their bicycles meant that they could not be constrained by clothing. It was about this time that the early form of the bra first appeared in Paris and London. The whole look of underwear was being revolutionized, as women finally tired of defining every inch and curve at the expense of their health and liberty. Women started wearing not so much a silhouette as a shift - easy to work and move in, but, more importantly, easy to dance in.

FLAPPER

The charleston and the tango required loose clothing, and the bright young things of the 1920s, energetic and irreverent, perfectly embodied the spirit of their times. Short hair, cigarettes and bare backs, as well as developments in fabrics and dyeing, called for a new attitude toward lingerie. No longer a prison that kept women from doing anything, undergarments became pretty, flirty and desirable. Perhaps this was the true start of women's love affair with lingerie, as for the first time they experienced sensuous fabrics close to the skin that were comfortable, yet supportive.

The guiding influence behind the 'garçon' look was Coco Chanel. In contrast to the mature, womanly shape of the previous decade, she laid the foundation for a lean, boyish silhouette. Her style was a reaction to the blowsy, over-decorated Belle Époque. Originally a milliner, Chanel began designing when customers who bought her hats asked for copies of her own dresses, but her rise to fame started during the war when opulence was impossible and practicality essential. Chanel herself loved the outdoor life and elegance combined with freedom of movement was what was most important to her in terms of fashion. She

Right: Magazines of the early 1900s carried various adverts and illustrations extolling the merits of different forms of corsetry and undergarments.

redefined the feminine image, making it more simple and more masculine, using innovative fabrics such as soft, supple jersey and influences from British men's tailoring and sportswear.

Though women had worn trousers during the war, the fashion world had paid little heed, considering them uniforms. However, Chanel promoted trousers, designing them loose, ankle-length and high-waisted. She did not really use foundation, and without it women had to be thin or lithe for the clothes to look flattering. Some suggest that by changing the form in this way Chanel started the cult of the thin woman in fashion. Nevertheless, the importance of her contribution cannot be underestimated.

Our modern image of the flapper is of a dizzy young woman in a glittering beaded shift shimmying to jazz music. Unfortunately, the truth is that the 1920s silhouette looked terrible on most women, totally ignoring their curves and dropping the waist to the widest point of the body, the hips. The roll-on and the suspender belt enjoyed a popularity that means they are still available today, but not so the formless masculine silhouette. By the early 1930s, the flapper look had died out, and once again women turned to underwear to reinstate their natural curves. Although the overall silhouette remained narrow, fashion returned to femininity by accentuating breasts and hips, achieved by cutting dresses on the bias. To maintain the slim, flowing line, women wore less underneath than ever before. Camiknickers, a camisole with French knickers, along with brassieres and girdles, were the order of the day. Never before had so much pressure been put on the body to achieve the fashionable form, as opposed to foundation, which previously had done all the work.

97

FLOWER WOMEN AND SWEATER GIRLS

'Without foundation there can be no fashion.' Christian Dior

Those of us without direct experience of the effect the Second World War had on everyday life tend to take the creativity of those years for granted. Today, wars can and do take place all over the world, yet we remain totally unaffected. At that time, nylon was scarce, so with characteristic ingenuity women would draw seams on their legs to imitate stockings and use parachute silk to make underclothes. The fashions of the war years were intensely practical. Square shoulders, short skirts and trousers gave women a uniformed, military look, which made them appear very proper and busy, working for 'the cause'. All fabrics and clothing were strictly rationed, and as it took three clothing coupons just to buy a pair of knickers, fashion had to make do without form. The end of the war did not bring an end to rationing, and in the midst of this austere atmosphere Christian Dior launched his New Look.

The skimpy masculine fashions of post-war Europe revolted Dior, who longed for women to regain the charm and femininity of his mother's era. It has been said that he wanted to change the female form, and to truly innovate in fashion, the form must change, a different set of proportions must be achieved. To counter the straight-down shape of the previous 20 years, Dior returned to structure. At its launch in 1947, his New Look caused shock waves all over the world, provoking reactions from

Opposite: Manassés' vision of the roaring 1920s – shiny silk stockings, cropped hair and cigarettes.

Above: All the fun of the fair, London 1938.

adoration to disgust. Dissenters mostly protested at the amount of fabric Dior used in his full skirts, but admirers celebrated the fact that curves were back.

The New Look offered an image of women as flowers: slim stems from the waist up preceded huge skirts like open blooms. The silhouette could only be achieved by wearing either a waspie to cinch in the waist or a special corset with padding on the hips. Many of Dior's evening dresses transcended the barrier between fashion and foundation by incorporating the corsetry within their structure. Some dresses were so finely constructed that they would stand up on their own. By way of example, think of Marilyn Monroe singing DIAMONDS ARE A GIRL'S BEST FRIEND and moving her body from side to side while her fabulous pink gown stays in exactly the same place!

Dior padded the hips and the bodice to emphasize curves. Each skirt was first lined with tulle for shape, and then with fine silk to prevent stockings from laddering. Each dress or suit was sold

Right: Sweater girl, Gina Lollobrigida.

Opposite: One of Dior's creations featured by **Vogue** in 1948 from the Envol, meaning 'take off' or 'flight', collection, which followed the New Look.

with the appropriate foundation garment; for example, a special boned corset to lift the breasts which was also flounced on the hips to create extra curves.

All this was very well, you might say, for those who could afford couture, but even with rationing, the New Look became incredibly desirable. Because women were desperate for glamour after the grim war years, Utility-clothing manufacturers translated Dior's designs for British department stores. The firm Dereta produced 700 New Look suits in grey flannel, which sold out in two weeks even though they were made of unrationed fabric and could not be repeated. Girls who could not afford the Utility copies or the more expensive versions improvised by adding old fabric to existing dresses to create the required fullness.

The foundation industry responded to demand by manufacturing short corsets called basques, waspies and bras. Although bras had become widely available in the mid-1930s, they really came into their own when the vogue for high, pointed breasts, started by Dior, gained momentum. Once again, the female form was exalted by lingerie. Bras with circular stitching gave the required 'torpedo' shape, while strapless bras became available to cope with strapless evening gowns and cocktail dresses. Inflatable bras to boost smaller cup sizes were widely advertised, though these were largely unreliable, as they tended to deflate noisily, or even explode at high altitudes!

The influence of Hollywood movies and boom-time America in the 1950s had a massive impact on the way women dressed. In a Europe yearning to escape the frugality of a long hard war, the all-American sweater girl provided one of the popular looks of the day. Whether wearing full skirts or tight pedal pushers, the waist was cinched and the breasts thrust out. The tight sweater was the perfect way for a girl to look womanly and well endowed and show what her push-out bra could do. Doris Day, Jayne Mansfield, Marilyn Monroe and Brigitte Bardot's feminine figures and luscious pouts inspired generations of sex kittens. The sex appeal of lingerie was prominently displayed, as movie stars flaunted their cleavages and the lingerie that enhanced them on the silver screen. Romance and glamour defined the fashionable look and some of the prettiest and sexiest corsetry was made around this time.

A FASHION EXPLOSION

The political climate at the end of the 1950s and the beginning of the 1960s brought fundamental changes for women in all aspects of their lives, not least in fashion. As already demonstrated, a new political climate demands a new silhouette. Epitomized by such models as Twiggy and Jean Shrimpton, this look was defined by the mini skirt, tunic dresses, and lots of bright colours and modern prints. Underwear followed suit, and matching bra and knicker sets, made of nylon and polyester, became available in sizzling colours. The figure-hugging nature of jeans and skirts gave birth to the bikini brief, and brief it certainly was, slung low on the hips and just covering the bottom with the barest of stretchy fabric. Tights were a new invention and solved the problem of what to wear under crotch-skimming skirts. Not surprisingly, tights did not really catch on at first, as stockings had been an integral part of feminine dress for centuries. However, comfort and practicality soon won women over, and legs became the new erogenous zone. Tights began to appear in all shades, fabrics and designs, thanks to the development of Lycra by Du Pont, which not only transformed hosiery, but lingerie in general.

Those at the forefront of the scene during the late 1960s and early 1970s encouraged a diversity of looks and styles, largely due to their heroic and self-confident attitudes. As a result, no one particular look defined this do-it-yourself era; fashion was about being as individual as possible. For example, in the heyday of Studio 54, women were shiny, slinky and glam. Wearing boob tubes and tight satin flares with as little underwear as possible, they showed off their figures to the best possible advantage.

From London to Paris, New York to San Francisco, this new generation found the perfect climate for creativity and self-expression. People were turning their own ideas concerning style and fashion into commercial enterprises. Providing that the ideas and the clothes were original and reflected the spirit of the time, success had never been so easy. At this point, fashion literally exploded. There were so many ideas, so many directions, that we decided to choose just some of the many examples of how underwear and foundation defined fashion.

The dance and exercise craze was one of the main influences on early 1980s fashion. Sporty underwear, like Calvin Klein's now-famous range, was based on men's underwear and was not really flattering to the form. Debbie Moore of Pineapple popularized the look of a healthy, active lifestyle with her collection, inspired by the dancers at her studio. The body-conscious could flaunt their toned muscles in skin-tight leotards and tights worn with legwarmers.

Designers such as Jean-Paul Gaultier, Thierry Mugler and John Galliano were beginning to experiment with corsetry and form as a fashion look. Much has been written about underwear as outerwear, or Madonna and her corsets, or Mugler's 'Built Like a Buick' metal construction, and for this reason we are not really interested in exploring these themes further. I want to talk about Vivienne Westwood, not only because she is my mum and I love her, but also because she is, without doubt, the most innovative designer in fashion and her work over the last 25 years has been an inspiration to all.

102

VIVE LA COCOTTE

...in the collections Erotic Zones and Vive la Cocotte, they [Vivienne and Andreas] achieved a new silhouette, extreme and incredible in this age of dressing down. I remember Naomi, Tatiana, Shalom – the first high steps set off an electric current running up those long fine legs, swinging the chassis, nipping the waist, pushing out the breasts and illuminating the gaze beneath toques and bonnets...of women who felt themselves adored.

Gene Krell, VIVIENNE WESTWOOD

The best place to start is in 1974. Vivienne Westwood and Malcolm McLaren renamed their Kings Road shop SEX and started selling S&M-style clothing as fashion. Rubberwear and leather skirts were worn with fishnets and stilettos, studs and torn T-shirts. The impact of these clothes, and the punk rockers who adopted them, forced people to reconsider what was attractive, sexy and beautiful. As punk descended into the caricature it is today, Vivienne and Malcolm made the catwalk a new showcase for their ideas, starting with their famous Pirates collection in 1981. The Buffalo collection in 1982, one of their last collaborations together, was based on a mixture of hobo and ethnic influences, and showed, for the first time, a bra worn over a dress. The design was inspired by Peruvian peasant women, who regarded the bra, an expensive luxury, as something that should be shown off to their community as a status symbol.

In 1984 Westwood introduced the mini-crini, combining the full hips and the swing of the crinoline with a modern mini length. When Sadie Frost modelled the now famous Westwood corset for the

Above: Sarah in Vivienne Westwood's first Stature of Liberty corset.

Harris Tweed collection of 1987, she was hailed with cries of 'come back, darling!' as she left the catwalk, leaving no doubt of the corset's utterly seductive power. The innovation of the corset lies in the stretch panels, closed with a zip, which makes the formerly rigid garment easy to wear and contemporary. The corset shapes the natural lines of the body into audaciously sexy curves. Like Dior before her, Westwood used the structure previously provided by underwear to create a sophisticated piece of clothing that makes the most of the female form. She named this corset Stature of Liberty, highlighting the status, freedom and power of the female form in the shape of a gorgeous and sexy woman. Never one to feel that women are victims of their circumstances, Westwood has promoted and enhanced the female form, showing it off in all its glory.

When Agent Provocateur opened in 1994, there were no new ideas in underwear. With a true love of fashion and glamour, we set about creating pieces that gave people the option to reawaken their desires. Quite unintentionally, we were instrumental in inspiring a whole stream of clothing to show off the lingerie, and I think this is a consequence of lingerie being ignored for so long. Hopefully, it will come round to the point where people will simply appreciate it for how it makes them feel under their clothes.

Chapter 5 Fantasy

'Let's do all the things we ever wanted to do or have done to us. We have the whole night. There are so many objects here that we can use. You have costumes too. I'll dress up for you… We will begin with your fantasies. We won't stop until we have realized them all.'

Anaïs Nin, DELTA OF VENUS

Fantasy is one of the most important parts of life, the aspect of sexuality that can be indulged in anywhere. There is no end to the diversity of the imagination, and no limit to which you may not go. Fantasy is not, by any means, confined to the imagination: it can refer to that which is fantastic, sensational and gorgeous. For many of us, the images that dominate sexual fantasies are people and situations that are totally different to our everyday surroundings. We can be transformed into wild creatures, dancing without inhibitions, lusciously decorated, with all eyes observing and desiring us.

Some fantasies are arousing in their very safety – sexy because they are so comforting and normal. They might involve people from everyday life: the man you see on the bus to work, a girl serving in a shop, a nurse or a policewoman who triggers the imagination to run wild with thoughts of what you would like to do with her. Sometimes the safest fantasies are those in which you are an observer, the powerless voyeur.

The most sexually interesting and arousing female fantasy figures – strippers, dancers, dominatrices, for example – are markedly different from the people we normally see around us. They command the maximum attention because they have 'exoticized' their bodies through costume and decoration, and they offer an open invitation for others to enter their fantasy world.

Dancing and lovemaking each inspire the other and share a common instrument – the human body. The arousal of dance can be enhanced in many ways – it inspires the primal feeling of losing oneself in movement and sensation, crossing all boundaries of language and culture.

110

Costumes, decorations and glittering accessories glorify the body. Tribal communities have always understood the importance of the transition from adolescence to adulthood and celebrate awakening sexuality through dance and by symbolically decorating the body with tattoos, paint, feathers and beads, as our ancestors once would have done. Somewhere deep in our psyche are embedded certain points of reference that are akin to these tribal customs and which we recognize as a 'come-on'. These universal signs can be seen in tassels swinging from tits, ankle and belly chains, and painted lips – all which draw attention to parts of the body that are sexually interesting.

In fantasy we can freely begin to explore the animal instinct, the drive towards the ultimate goal of pleasure. We no longer have to think rationally, but can be ruled by sensations, feelings and rhythms. Truth and reality are not important in fantasy: anything is possible. This chapter offers a selection of fantasies that show an endless array of possibilities. Some are mysterious, weird and exotic; some include the excitement of fear. Because we are not interested in what is 'socially acceptable' in terms of behaviour and language, we have chosen these particular excerpts for your enjoyment.

THE MISTRESS

Anna was extremely beautiful and quite stunning. Her ebony body was strapped into a skin harness, a pale, fine skin stretched over her dark skin like a drum, so tight it was like the inside of her own skin, as if, assuming the inside of her skin were white, she had been flayed, turned inside out and then sewn on to her own flesh in the places where the costume was.

For everything she wore had been cut out of this skin: her elbow-length gloves, her corset tight around her waist, gripping her breasts below the nipples, her tiny pants which were so closely welded to her crack that it looked even more thoroughly obscene than if she were naked, and even her thigh-length boots…which she wore like stockings, went as far up as the tops of her thighs where they were attached to her corset by suspenders which were also made of skin…

Yet the most gripping, chilling aspect of Anna's get-up was not any of this, but the objects which served as her headdress and belt. She had stuck over her head, after tying back the abundant mass of hair which fell down her back, a stuffed hyena's head, with its jaws open and its lips curled back over yellow fangs, which could only have looked more vividly real if it had started barking. Around her waist she had tied a cord of hemp whose two ends fell down between her legs where they were attached to a pair of scissors, pointing downwards, like a man's sex, with two small testicles and a penis of steel, hanging beneath her own female sex so tightly clad in the skin.

Anna stood there immobile, regal…in an explicitly dominant pose. 'Didn't I forbid you to have pleasure without me?' she pronounced, in a voice in which softness contended with malice.

'Yes mistress.'

Alina Reyes, BEHIND CLOSED DOORS

THE SLAVE

One of the most famous erotic novels of all is THE STORY OF O by Pauline Réage. It is a love story of submission to pleasure and pain.

Midway up one of the library's walls ran a balcony supported by two pillars. In one of these, as high up as a man standing on tiptoe could reach, was sunk a hook. O, whose lover had taken her in his arms, one hand under her shoulder, the other in her womb which was burning her almost unbearably, O was informed that when, as soon as they would, they unfastened her hands, it would only be to attach them to this whipping post by means of the bracelets on her wrists and this steel chain. With the exception of her hands, which would be immobilized a little above her head, she would be able to move, to turn, to face around and see the strokes coming, they told her; by and large, they'd confine the whipping to her buttocks and thighs, to the space, that is to say, between her waist and her knees, precisely that part of her which had been prepared in the car when she had been made to sit naked on the seat; it was likely, however, that some of the four men would want to score her with the crop, for it caused fine, long, deep welts which lasted quite some time.

Pauline Réage, THE STORY OF O

THE CANCAN

They come in from all sides, the girls. They are shaking their skirts and screaming with excitement. The music is frantic as they form a semicircle, their skirts raised to their shoulders like great wide mouths, their legs kicking higher and higher. Everyone is straining for a glimpse of flesh, eyes devouring the tops of thighs above tight garters, which hold up fishnet stockings, looking for gaps in the frills of knickers. As quickly as they came, they leave, one doing the splits with her legs spread as wide as possible in midair, while another bends over and with an impudent flick of her skirts shows you her bottom before running to follow the rest.

THE AFRICAN GOD

In this excerpt from DELTA OF VENUS, three characters, Elena, Bijou and Leila, consult Bijou's African clairvoyant, who has promised to dance for them. The story ends with them all dancing and making love.

His dance for the women took place one evening... He stripped himself, showing his gleaming golden-brown body. To his waist he tied a fake penis modelled like his own and the same colour.

He said, 'This is a dance from my own country. We do this for the women on feast days.' In the

114

dimly lit room...he began to move his belly... He jerked his body as if entering a woman and simulated the spasms of a man caught in...an orgasm. The final spasm was wild, like a man giving up his life in the act of sex.

The three women watched. At first only the fake penis dominated, but then the real one, in the heat of the dance, began to compete in length and weight. Now they both moved in rhythm with his gestures... The effect on Bijou was powerful. She took her dress off. She began to dance around him temptingly. But he merely touched her now and then with the tip of his sex, wherever he encountered her, and continued to turn and jerk his body in space like a savage dancing against an invisible body.

The teasing affected Elena, too, and she slipped her dress off and kneeled near them, just to be in the orbit of their sexual dance. She suddenly wanted to be taken until she bled, by this big, strong, firm penis dangled in front of her, as he performed a male danse du ventre, with its tantalizing motions.

Now Leila, who did not desire men, became caught up by the moods of the two women and tried to embrace Bijou, but Bijou would not have it. She was fascinated with the two penises.

Leila tried to kiss Elena also. Then she rubbed her nipples against both women, trying to entice them. She pressed herself against Bijou to profit from her excitement, but Bijou continued to concentrate on the male organs dangled before her. Her mouth was open, and she, too, was dreaming of being taken by a double-sexed monster who could satisfy her two centres of response at once.

Anaïs Nin, DELTA OF VENUS

115

THE EXHIBITIONIST

I have tremendous exhibitionist urges... I'd love to perform a strip act which culminated in [me] fucking the whole damn male audience...

I'd love to be seeing a porno film in a theatre - I can feel and see myself getting hot and wet because the film is really turning me on. All of a sudden, I feel a strange hand on my thigh slowly heading for my black tiny bikini panties. The hand has reached its mark and finds me wet and ready... I remove the panties, and he opens his fly. I move over and sit on his lap thereby causing his 12-inch-long sex tool to go easily and smoothly into my burning sex hole - up and down I go till we exhaust ourselves in climax. Then we part and he moves to a different location in the darkened theatre. I've never seen his face...

Nancy Friday, ed., FORBIDDEN FLOWERS, ROXANNE'S FANTASY

THE SCHOOLGIRL

She had black silk stockings on covering her knees, but I was unable to see as far up as the cunt (this name, which I always used with Simone, is, I think, by far the loveliest of the names for the vagina). It merely struck me that by slightly lifting the pinafore from behind I might see her private parts unveiled.

Now in the corner of the hallway there was a saucer of milk for the cat. 'Milk is for the pussy isn't it?' said Simone. 'Do you dare me to sit in the saucer?'

'I dare you,' I answered, almost breathless.

The day was extremely hot. Simone put the saucer on a small bench, planted herself before me, and, with her eyes fixed on me, she sat down without my being able to see her burning buttocks under the skirt, dipping into the cool milk. The blood shot to my head, and I stood before her awhile, immobile and trembling, as she eyed my stiff cock bulging in my trousers. Then I lay down at her feet without her stirring, and for the first time, I saw her 'pink and dark' flesh cooling in the white milk. We remained motionless, both of us equally overwhelmed...

Georges Bataille, THE STORY OF THE EYE

THE STRIPPER/THE BELLY DANCER

The dance begins with a cry and I remember I cried so loudly my lover looked shocked. Then I began to take off my clothes, carefully one garment at a time. First I discard my shawl from my hips as soon as I begin to dance more vigorously, then my yelek, which the Americans call a waistcoat, so that my thin white shirt exposes my breasts, and as I dance my shirt clings to my body and I know that my body is teasing my lover. My girdle I throw at his feet and it falls heavily in his lap because it is embroidered with precious stones and with the ringing of my girdle still in my ears I take off my shintiya, which the Americans call trousers. All the time I continue to dance, moving my hips like a seesaw, altering the weight and balance of my body and shaking my breasts which become clearer through my shirt as the heat in the tent gets closer and closer. Finally I remove my shirt and, as I turn from my hips, my hair falls in his face and over his body again and again. All the time I continued to dance on my knees with my back bent over so my face looked up at his... When I was naked I began moving my stomach more and more violently and the musicians quickened their pace when they heard me crying shrilly in a high voice and they knew the dance was in its final frenzy... The dance is a very powerful dance and we made great love that evening many times I remember. Many times.

Lucinda Jarret, STRIPPING IN TIME: A HISTORY OF EROTIC DANCING

SIMONE AND MARCELLE

Simone also daydreamed about my holding Marcelle, this time with nothing on but her garter-belt and stockings, her cunt aloft, her legs bent, and her head down; Simone herself, in a bathrobe drenched in hot water and thus clinging to her body but exposing her bosom, would then get up on a white enamelled chair with a cork seat. I would arouse her breasts from a distance by lifting the tips on the heated barrel of a long service revolver that had been loaded and just fired... At the same time, she would pour a jar of dazzling white crème fraîche on Marcelle's grey anus, and she would also urinate freely in her robe, or if the robe were ajar, on Marcelle's back or head, while I could piss on Marcelle from the other side (I would certainly piss on her breasts). Furthermore, Marcelle herself could fully inundate me if she liked, for while I held her up, her thighs would be gripping my neck. And she could also stick my cock in her mouth and what not.

Georges Bataille, THE STORY OF THE EYE

THE KAMA-SUTRA

The KAMA-SUTRA is one of the earliest attempts in Hindu tradition to outline the relationship between men and women. At the core of this relationship is sexual love, and this is what the KAMA-SUTRA explores: who should make love to whom, and how, and under what circumstances. The book describes how to win a woman's heart, and how to give both partners the maximum of pleasure. Renowned for the hundreds of sexual positions depicted, the KAMA-SUTRA is beautifully written - sometimes romantically poetic, sometimes frank and instructive.

NAILMARKS AND LOVEBITES

Once passion is stirring,
lovers should bring their nails into play,
the effect is electrifying:
under a lady's nails even the most diffident lover
feels his body slowly charge with desire.

Nail-play is especially exciting
the first time lovers go to bed together;
on the nights before and after a long separation;
after a blazing row,
and when she's had a little too much to drink.

...When her nipple is caught
between five nails driving sharply together
in a sunburst of delicate red rays,
it is the famous Peacock's Foot -
difficult to make and prized highly by women.

If she shamelessly begs you
to make the Peacock's Foot upon her breast
and you, with five nails only,
score first one breast and then the other,
it is the virtuoso Leap of a Hare.

KAMA-SUTRA

The Nurse

...I was hospitalized in the hospital in which I worked as a registered nurse. There were two doctors who came by on a daily basis to examine me. They were both quite arrogant and domineering in their mannerisms. As they examined me, they would have me remove my gown and have a great time poking around the most intimate parts of my body.

After they left the room, I fantasized that they were the patients, and I was the nurse in charge of them. My first order was to have them remove their clothing and put on one of those backless hospital gowns while I watched their every move. Next, I positioned them on an examination table and strapped their feet into the table's metal stirrups. In this position, I have a perfect view of their rears and penises. Since I'm wearing a short skirt with no underwear, I constantly bend over in order to expose myself to them, causing huge erections. After inserting a well-lubricated finger in their rears, I masturbate each of them until they ejaculate. By this time, they are begging me to continue...

Nancy Friday, ed., FORBIDDEN FLOWERS, MOREEN'S FANTASY

Fruits of Pleasure

The lovely young men surrounded her, rubbing the golden oil into her skin, smiling down at her as they worked...she saw a brush dipping down to colour her nipples carefully with glittering gold pigment. She was too shocked to make a sound. She lay still as her lips were also painted. The soft hairs of the brush skilfully lined her eyes with the gold, stroking it on to her eyelashes. Great jewelled earrings were shown to her and, with a little gasp, she felt her earlobes stabbed... The earrings dangled from the tiny burning wounds and the pain dissolved as she felt her legs drawn apart and a bowl of brightly coloured, glistening fruits was held above her...

And she saw that he was taking the fruit from the bowl - dates, pieces of melon and peach, tiny pears, dark red berries - and that he was carefully dipping each piece in a silver cup of honey. Her legs stretched wide apart and she realized the honeyed fruit was being placed inside of her... She couldn't keep from moaning, but her captors seemed to approve... She was filled with the fruit. She felt it bulging from her. And now she was shown the glistening bunch of ripe grapes that was laid between her legs...her underarms were being painted thickly with honey. And something, a plump date perhaps, was being pressed into her navel. Jewelled bracelets went about her wrists. She was being fitted with heavy anklets. She undulated almost irresistibly on the pillow as the tension mounted in her, the vague infatuation with the smiling faces. And she knew fear, too, as she felt herself transformed into an astonishing ornament.

Anne Rice, BEAUTY'S PUNISHMENT

The Carnaval

I am standing on a balcony high above the Carnaval. The Salvador air is warm and sultry. I can see bodies below me glistening with sweat, dancing to the rhythm of the pounding drums. A parade goes past, and the girl leading them is dressed in a skirt of swaying grasses and nothing else - her breasts are painted with glitter and they mesmerize me as they swing and sway to the beat. I am taking it all in, my body pressed against the stone of the balcony. Earlier this evening I was dancing in the square wearing my bikini and a tiny pair of shorts that showed the cheeks of my

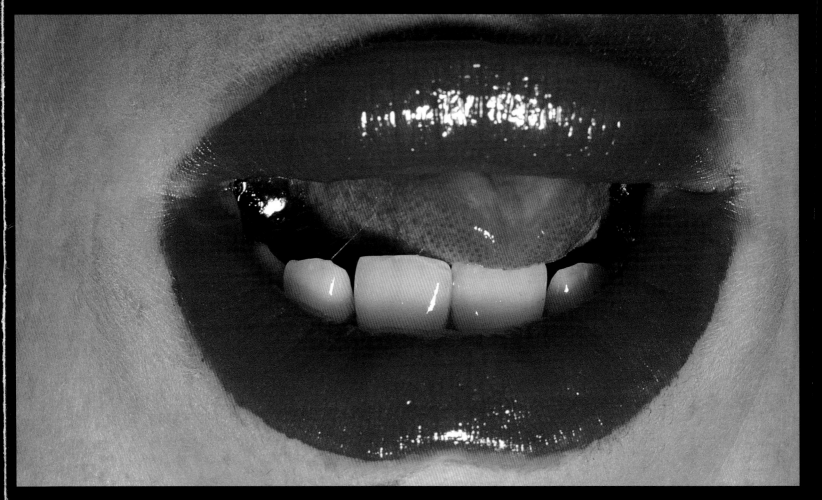

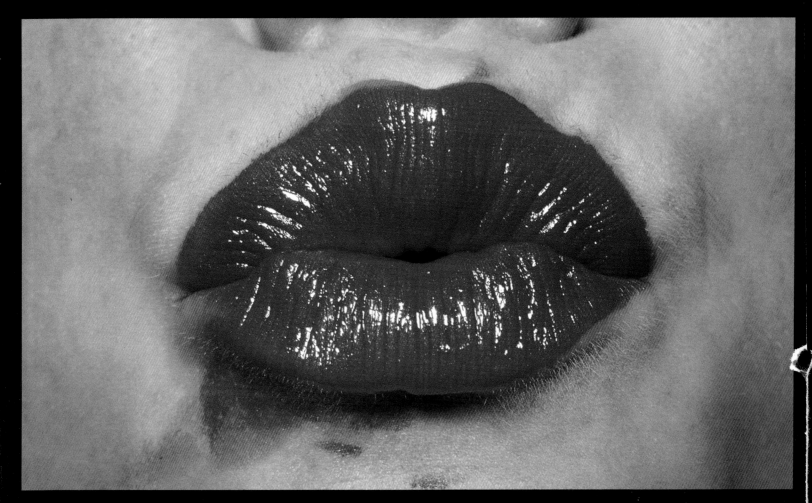

KODAK

26 ▷ 26A

ass. Hands were touching me everywhere, not the hands of my partner, that anonymous man who led me into the samba, our bodies melting together like we were making love. I am watching thousands of people in the square below me dancing out their fantasies, flaunting their bodies with abandon. As I lean over, he enters me from behind, in time with the rhythm of the drums, and I come so quickly, with the drums in my head and the sequins of the dancers shimmering before my eyes. I am coming so hard and it's the last night of Carnaval, and this is the physical sensation of the joy that makes you high and I am watching it all - the movement and the rhythm and the energy of it and I am screaming and I forget myself and this is it, the Carnaval, this is it...

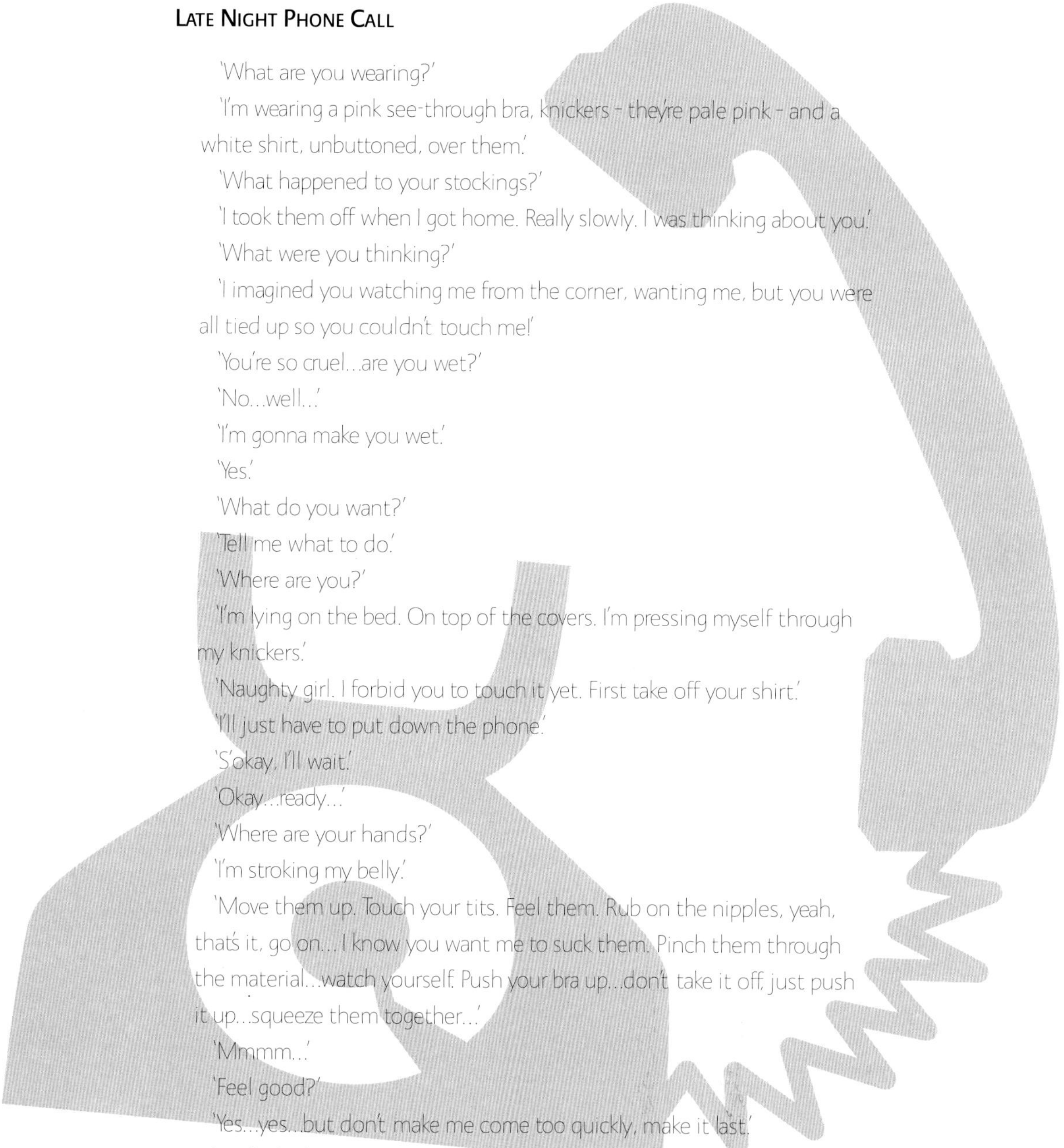

LATE NIGHT PHONE CALL

'What are you wearing?'

'I'm wearing a pink see-through bra, knickers - they're pale pink - and a white shirt, unbuttoned, over them.'

'What happened to your stockings?'

'I took them off when I got home. Really slowly. I was thinking about you.'

'What were you thinking?'

'I imagined you watching me from the corner, wanting me, but you were all tied up so you couldn't touch me.'

'You're so cruel...are you wet?'

'No...well...'

'I'm gonna make you wet.'

'Yes.'

'What do you want?'

'Tell me what to do.'

'Where are you?'

'I'm lying on the bed. On top of the covers. I'm pressing myself through my knickers.'

'Naughty girl. I forbid you to touch it yet. First take off your shirt.'

'I'll just have to put down the phone.'

'S'okay, I'll wait.'

'Okay...ready...'

'Where are your hands?'

'I'm stroking my belly.'

'Move them up. Touch your tits. Feel them. Rub on the nipples, yeah, that's it, go on... I know you want me to suck them. Pinch them through the material...watch yourself. Push your bra up...don't take it off, just push it up...squeeze them together...'

'Mmmm...'

'Feel good?'

'Yes...yes...but don't make me come too quickly, make it last.'

'I will, don't worry...you know it's all for you. We can talk all night.'

124

I could hear her screaming with pleasure...

I made him...

HE ASKED ME IF I WOULD EVER...

THE MATTRESS WAS FILTHY...

He called me and started to tell me...

I thought I was dreaming when I felt...

He made me watch them through a hole in the wall...

The door was just open enough for me to see...

I LOVE IT WHEN...

And then he told me he'd like to...

I took him to a room full of mirrors...

THE WAY SHE WAS TIED MEANT THAT HE COULD...

HE PUSHED ME INTO THE STINKING CUBICLE AND CLOSED THE DOOR...

and then the three of them...

T H E N   I   F E L T   H I M ....

She moved closer to...

She started to remove her silky panties

WHAT IF HE...

The sand got everywhere when we...

I'm going out tonight, what shall I wear...

When I turned around...

IT WAS SO DARK IN THE CLUB THAT NO ONE COULD SEE US....

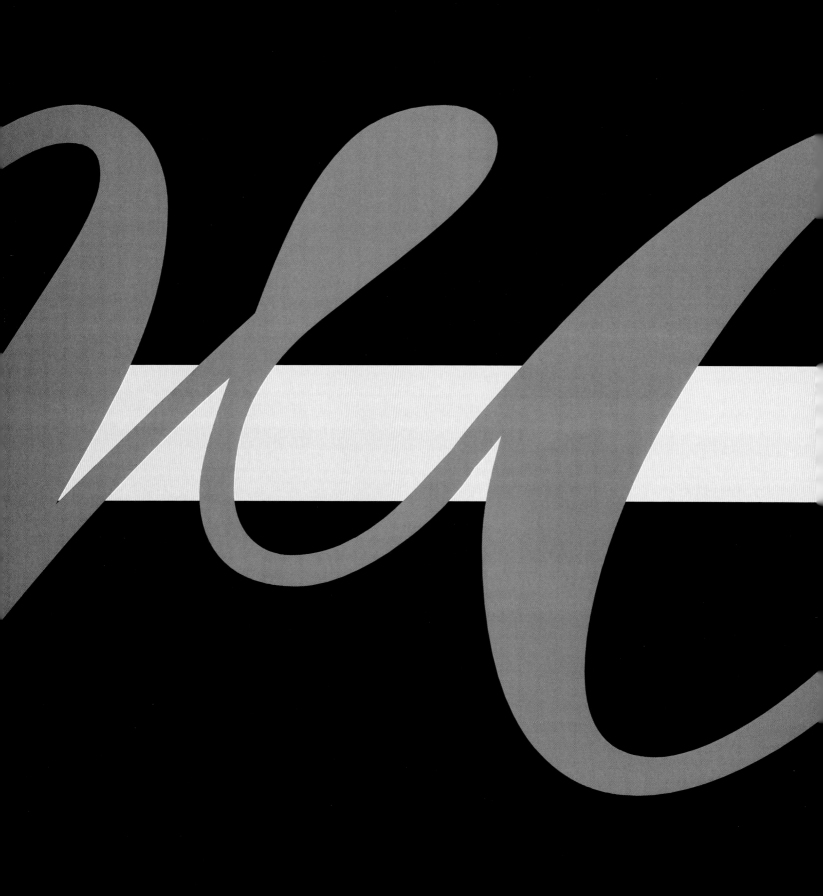

Chapter 6 Striptease

> 'You have to have a reason, a story, when you take your clothes off. You can't just take them off.'
>
> Dixie Evans

The idea of a beautiful woman dancing and taking her clothes off is certainly one of the simplest yet most exciting fantasies, and the one that is probably the most universally appealing.

IN THE BEGINNING...

The earliest, and perhaps most famous, striptease is said to belong to Salome, daughter of Herodias. In return for the head of John the Baptist, Salome performed the seductive Dance of the Seven Veils for the delight of Herod and his court. Her striptease was immortalized by Oscar Wilde in his play SALOMÉ and the Strauss opera of the same name. Canadian-born Maud Allan, one of the earliest known erotic dancers, scandalized Western society by performing a dance called Visions of Salome, wearing a sheer skirt and a bodice made entirely of beads. A review of her 1906 performance shows how she combined the fantasy of the Orient with a powerful female sexuality:

130

> Her naked feet, slender and arched, beat a sexual measure. The pink pearls slip amorously about her bosom and throat as she moves, while the long strand of jewels that floats from the belt about her waist floats languorously apart from her smooth hips. The desire that flames from her eyes and bursts in hot flames from her scarlet mouth infects the very air with the madness of passion. Swaying like a witch with yearning hands and arms that plead, Miss Allan is such a delicious embodiment of lust that she might win forgiveness with the sins of such wonderful flesh...

Lucinda Jarret, STRIPPING IN TIME: A HISTORY OF EROTIC DANCING

Right: Cheeky striptease at the Crazy Horse Saloon in Paris.

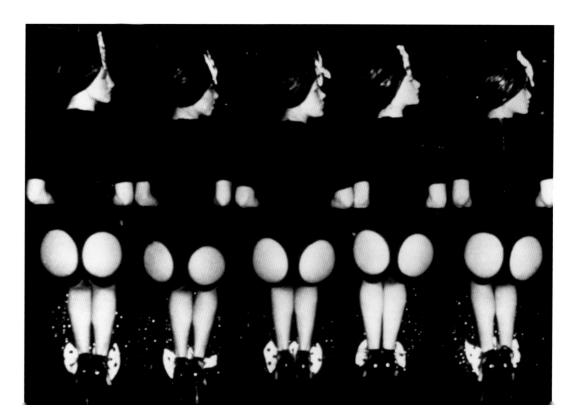

One of the first stage acts to feature showgirls was started by Lydia Thompson and her British Blondes, who entranced America with their saucy routines in 1868. The girls had a direct relationship with their audience, making them the precursors of the genre of American striptease artists who continue to be successful throughout their lives for their charm and individuality as well as their striptease skills. Long before the striptease became popular in America, however, one of its predecessors was kicking up a storm in Europe. Known variously as polka-piqué, Robert Macaire and chahut, the dance is most famously known as French Cancan.

THE FRENCH CANCAN

Forget the image of a saucy chorus line in white frillies: that is the fin-de-siècle gentrification for tourists of what, in the 1860s, was a sexually predatory ritual, open to all comers, in which most women went knickerless, flashing glimpses of their genitals to men, challenging them to thrust and enter, as the dance became hotter, faster, louder.

Rupert Christianson,

TALES OF THE NEW BABYLON: PARIS IN THE MID-NINETEENTH CENTURY

The origins of the cancan are somewhat obscure, and the dance seems to have evolved rather than appeared in the form we recognize today. Cancan started in 1830s Paris as an amateur dance where couples performed a sort of galop together, improvised with high kicks and other wild movements. The dance was frenzied, sexually exciting and largely indulged in by the lower classes and 'loose' women. For 30 years or so, the cancan was dominated by men, both as a performance and as a public pastime. But as the scandalous high kicks and splits became further exaggerated, the dance became much more interesting when performed by women.

The first really famous cancaneuses appeared in Second-Empire Paris, around 1850. The artistes Rigolboche and Finette performed wild, uninhibited cancan on the dance floor, sometimes in male costume, but more often in the froth of petticoats and frilly lingerie so beloved of the period. As yet, suspenders were not worn, and stockings were held up with garters below long white bloomers. Nevertheless, the dance was considered outrageously provocative, especially when Finette incorporated the grand écart – splits performed high in the air. Both French and foreign audiences were absolutely delighted with the cancan and would roar their applause for each flash of lace beneath the skirt. At the Bal Mabille, the girls would dance with their skirts raised to their shoulders, exposing their stockings and knickers. However, should a gentleman stick his face too close to the inviting object, a swift high kick would knock his hat off and bring him to his senses, to the raucous amusement of the other spectators. The dance was characterized by its joie de vivre. The spirit of the dance would possess its participators until they were exhausted and could dance no more. The dancers also performed at the notorious masked bals publiques of the 1860s, held at the Paris Opéra, where men attended in evening dress but women were required to be masked or in costume. The carefree bals symbolized the extravagance and capacity for enjoyment of the Second Empire, which was to come to an abrupt and depressing end when the French were defeated by Prussia at the Battle of Sedan in 1870. When the German army arrived in Paris, they ushered in a decade of austerity and uncertainty, which was to see an inevitable backlash when the cancan was revived, bigger, better and saucier than ever!

132

Opposite: La Goulue – the most notorious cancaneuse of all time.

LA GOULUE

The main player in the cancan's revival was Louise Weber, better known as La Goulue, or the Glutton, the most famous cancaneuse of all time. Originally a laundress by profession, Louise came across elaborate and exciting lingerie owned by her upper-class customers. She would 'borrow' items and attend dances in the halls of Montmartre, showing off the lingerie to her admirers. When she realized that gentlemen would pay handsomely for the privilege of watching her dance, she began to perform publicly at the Elysée Montmartre, the main dance venue in Paris prior to the opening of the Moulin Rouge.

Above: A poster created for the Moulin Rouge by Toulouse-Lautrec, who was an ardent admirer of both the cancan and its performers.

Louise Weber was a fascinating subject for artists and photographers, and was inordinately proud of her body. Surviving prints show her dressed for the cancan, or in various erotic poses, sometimes completely nude, legs spread, and with a glass of champagne in one hand and a pipe in the other. On stage at the Moulin Rouge, she would sometimes appear bare-breasted in stationary tableaux. It was at the newly opened Moulin Rouge that La Goulue added another now-famous movement to the cancan. Towards the end of the dance, she would bend forward and toss her skirts over her head to reveal an embroidered heart on her bottom!

The Moulin Rouge opened in 1889 and heralded the arrival of the Naughty Nineties, with the cancaneuse as its representative. Immortalized by Toulouse-Lautrec, the Moulin Rouge became an enduring attraction of Paris and the place to see this spectacular dance. Jane Avril was one of Toulouse-Lautrec's favourite models, and the only dancer at the club permitted to wear coloured underwear. She would create fantastic costumes of graduating colours. One blood-red gown, for example, slowly faded in colour, petticoat by petticoat, ending in delicate pink knickers. Knickers were a cause of much controversy, especially for La Goulue who was fully aware of the sensation she could cause by showing her private parts. Though knickers at this time were generally two 'legs' attached to a waistband, and therefore open at the crotch, the management of the Moulin Rouge tried their best to ensure this gap was securely sewn. La Goulue had other ideas, as writer Georges Montorgeuil describes:

...[she tried] every possible way of showing what she should not and worse. She provokes by displaying her bare flesh as far as it can be seen amongst the magnificent jumble of her underwear, intentionally allowing a liberal amount of naked skin to be visible between her garter and the first flounce of her knickers, which slide up when she extends her leg. The transparent material barely covers the rest. She observes the fascination this provokes, gradually stirring it up through movements each more risqué than the last, and encouraging unhealthy curiosity to stretch to frantic searching, making the most of the effects of shadows in the pink areas glimpsed through gaps in the lace.

David Price, CANCAN!

With or without knickers, the cancan was considered more erotic than the *tableaux vivants* in which women would pose nude or semi-nude in a scene from popular mythology. Newspaper writers pointed out that it was the swirling of petticoats and the profusion of lingerie that made the dance so suggestive and alluring. The chorus line of girls, which is what most people associate with the cancan, was quite rare in France and was almost certainly an American invention. The solo stars at the Moulin Rouge usually danced on the floor at eye level, not on a stage, and their dance was less choreographed and more spontaneous than the chorus line.

As the 1890s drew to a close, the cancan had evolved, more or less, into the dance that we recognize today. Influences from America and even England had transformed it into a highly sophisticated performance, and one that became a symbol of national identity for the French. The cancan's popularity at the Moulin Rouge meant that the club became known as the home of the French Cancan and attracted audiences from all over the world, from ordinary people to the most famous movie stars of the day. The fundamental 'teasing' nature of the dance is what links it to striptease. While the cancan retains its glamorous element today, perhaps more strongly than ever, sadly the same cannot be said about striptease.

SWINGING TASSLES AND A SEQUINED G-STRING

The heyday of striptease began in America during the 1930s and continued well into the 1950s. Although there are many myths as to how it actually started, striptease reached the height of its popularity as the main attraction of burlesque shows. Some credit the Minsky brothers of New York with the invention of glamorous striptease. The star attraction in their variety shows at the Winter Garden theatre was the shy stripper. She would leave the stage for the first time still wearing her bra and knickers, then return to show off swinging tassels and a sequinned G-string (so called because it is the thinnest string on a violin), before leaving, with the audience howling for more. Louis Minsky was the one who discovered

INSTRUCTIONS
Cut out the figure, clothing, etc. on heavy lines. Fold tabs and flaps as needed. This doll should be assembled quickly, then undressed at a leisurely pace. However, do NOT remove clothing beyond bra and panties in city of Boston.

Stripper doll by Wally Wood, 1960s.

Rose Louise, better known as Gypsy Rose Lee, the woman who went down in history for the accomplishment of her act. Called the queen of 'sophisticated effect', Rose would, with a deadpan face, recite lines of verse as she removed her clothes:

When I raise my skirts with slyness and dexterity,
I'm mentally computing how much I'll give to charity
And though my thighs I have revealed
And just a little bit of me remains concealed
I'm thinking of the life of Duse.
Or the third chapter of The Rise and Fall of the Roman Empire.
When I lower my gown a fraction,
And expose a patch of shoulder,
I'm not thinking of your reaction,
I'm not even feeling colder.
I'm thinking of a landscape by Van Gogh or The Apples by Cézanne.
Or the charm I found in reading Lady Windermere's Fan...
Do you believe for one moment I'm thinking of sex?
Well, I certainly am...

The Minskys also pioneered the runway stage - an idea that Abe Minsky took from the Folies Bergères in Paris. By parading the girls on a runway, the audience was able to come closer to them than ever before, becoming intoxicated by the smell of perfume, sweat and the warmth of the girls' bodies as they performed floor work. The audiences could barely control their excitement at seeing the girls so closely and would often call out encouragement or abuse, trying to get the attention of the performers. The girls themselves would sometimes cheekily answer them back. As one story goes, a man shouted to the stripper on stage that he would really like to fuck her, and she, not missing a beat, naughtily wagged her finger at him saying, 'If you do, and I find out...!'

The Winter Garden venue was frequently hounded and under threat of closure from the public or the National League of Decency for crimes of immorality. In the most famous court case against the Minskys, the records show that the brothers challenged the narrow views of society and caused the charges to be dropped, but that so much free publicity resulted in sell-out shows. The brothers were finally forced out of New York in 1937, leaving behind them a string of dull imitations. It was not until after the Second World War that the new meccas of striptease arose. New Orleans, Las Vegas and San Francisco became the capitals of the 'golden age' of striptease, and their queen was Lilli St Cyr.

Opposite and below: Celluloid Striptease - Rita Hayworth in **GILDA**, 1946, and Valerie Perrine in **LENNY**, 1974.

THE FLYING G-STRING

Lilli St Cyr never plays to the audience or to individuals in the audience like most strippers do. Lilli is always the heroine in an exotic and sensual story that she has staged to identify with. Each guy can believe himself up there with her alone, so he's silent, attentive and respectful until the end of the story, and then the curtain brings him back to reality.

Peter de Cenzie

Lilli St Cyr made her debut at the Music Box in San Francisco as part of Russian producer Ivan Fevnova's company. Fevnova was well respected, so Lilli bluffed her audition using her wits and the incredible beauty of her 6-foot 2-inch body. The only problem was that she did not really know how to dance. Her debut was a complete disaster, and Fevnova was ready to fire her until he overheard a conversation between two fishermen who had seen her performance. Inspiration struck, and that night Lilli appeared in a routine called the Flying G-string. She danced to the top of a staircase, whereupon her G-string was whipped off by means of a fishing rod in the wings. As soon as it was gone, the lights fell and Lilli left the stage, protected by darkness. Fevnova trained her, and with her fame thus assured, she hired a team of designers and dressmakers who created fantastic and elegant costumes - robes with yards of tulle fabric, fur wraps and tight full-length evening gowns. Soon, important clubs began to compete for her, giving her top billing and paying up to $3800 a week for her to undress. It was at one such club, Ciro's, that she first performed her famous Bubble Bath routine. The stage was set as the boudoir of a rich and fashionable lady. Lilli would appear in a Dior gown and a fur stole and slowly undress before stepping into a transparent bath in just her tanga and a pair of shiny tassels. She also reversed this routine so that she

138

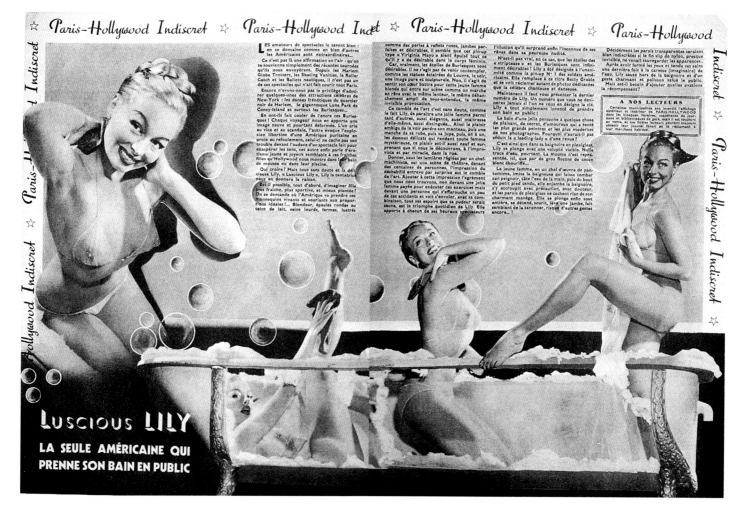

finished it completely dressed. The routine perfectly illustrates that striptease is not about taking all your clothes off, but the suspense involved in using the clothes slowly, to hide and reveal the body. Striptease is about the excitement of the movements you make, the poses you adopt to remove a skirt or put on a coat. It was at this that Lilli excelled.

A GLAMOROUS AGE

Lilli St Cyr was the most celebrated striptease artist of her time and a powerful influence on other girls in the industry. As Dixie Evans, the 'Marilyn Monroe' of striptease, says, 'She was the most flawless performer ever; everyone looked up to her'. Dixie started working in burlesque theatre in the early 1950s, and went on to become a famous performer. Far from being embarrassed about her past, she discusses her career with enthusiasm. Now in her 60s, she runs Exotic World, a museum in California opened by another stripper, the late Jenny Lee. 'It's important that these fabulous girls are not forgotten,' she says.

Dixie was always a dreamer, and as a child her imagination was filled with images from Hollywood movie magazines. At that time the craze was for the cutesy Shirley Temple, and Dixie managed to get free dancing lessons in return for teaching a few basic steps to the precocious offspring of mothers who nurtured their own Hollywood ambitions. She had a job pin-up modelling, and says that, though the girls were sometimes nude, the modelling was never explicit. Even so, she had to tell her family she was modelling for the Sears-Roebuck catalogue!

In San Francisco, broke, and with no way home, Dixie decided to try striptease. She was directed to a club near the theatre where she had been working as a page, and went downstairs to a basement room. 'I'll never forget it,' she says. There was Sandra Karina, dressed in nothing but a big white cowboy hat and boots shooting a pair of pistols from a holster round her waist while a room full of service men cheered her on. 'It looked really scary, but it turns out that they were the nicest bunch of girls and we all stuck together.' This was a glamorous age. Though girls who were starting out made their own costumes, those who were more famous would have designers come to them with ideas for acts based on their designs. Often, the in-house stripper would have a sewing machine and would make up costumes for other girls if they brought the materials. Costumes were a vital part of the act. As well as exciting lingerie and pasties covering the nipples, the girls would wear a full costume of some kind - often full-length beaded gowns, long gloves and a fur stole. They would also have elaborate props on stage. Dixie had an MGM movie set, complete with director's chair, camera and clapperboard.

The first item removed during the striptease was the glove. 'You would have to smile, and wink, and then slowly take the little finger of the glove and pull it off, each finger, one by one, and then you'd take the glove and lightly caress the top of someone's head before discarding it, and then each part of each little garment would take time,' Dixie remembers. 'You had to give the audience lots of attention and keep their attention.' Acts included girls who came out of oyster shells, bubble baths, teenage bedroom scenes, Hollywood scenes and dancing routines - each one was different. 'There was a huge variety of girls, and all of them were so individual that their acts were all really well received,' remembers Dixie.

Obviously, there was competition between the stars to come up with new and entertaining ideas. An immense amount of creativity went into planning each production and the details of it.

140

Not only did the movements of the striptease need to be worked out, but also the costumes, sets, music and the lighting.

WITH FLAMES RISING FROM HER CROTCH

At this time, striptease stars were well known for their individual personalities and specific routines. The outrageous Tempest Storm, who starred with Betty Page in the movie TEASARAMA for Irving Klaw, regularly wore a diamond-studded G-string. Cat Girl, Lilly Christine's most scandalous routine, involved miming sexual acts dressed in a pair of frilly see-through knickers and carrying a parasol. Lilly also performed a Voodoo Dance in an off-the-shoulder leopard-print dress, which was so erotic that the police asked her to tone it down for the sake of the audience, who were in danger of cardiac arrest! Blaze Starr, another famous stripper, enacted a routine while lying on a couch with artificial flames rising from her crotch. Zorita, known as the Blonde Bombshell, performed simulated sex with a live python. The girls sent their audiences into raptures, each getting a different response, from wide-eyed awe, like little boys in sweet shops for Lilli St Cyr, to yells of excitement and hats thrown in the air as Tempest tormented them in the final moments of her act.

All the girls had stage names, very much like the cancan dancers of earlier times. The names not only gave them added 'star quality', but also gave each girl a distinct, instantly recognizable persona. Dorian Dennis was known as Double Dynamite for her 39-inch bust. Tana Louise was the sophisticated Society Stripper. Mystery Girl was Jenny Adair, who performed in a mask, and Pepper Powell was dubbed Miss TNT In addition to their glamorous stage names, the most famous stars were described with equally flamboyant nicknames. Tempest Storm was the Shape that Shook the World, Lilli St Cyr was the Anatomic Bomb, while Blaze Starr was Miss Spontaneous Combustion. These explosive combinations were all part of the exaggerated world of burlesque, with its rowdy humour full of innuendo.

There is an art to taking your clothes off well, in an elegant yet seductive way. This is not to say that some of the acts were not raunchy, but the fact is that no one actually taught the girls how to strip. The artists may have had pointers from agents or managers, but stripping was all about watching each other, finding music 'that really turned you on' and lots of practice in front of a mirror. When asked what makes a great stripper, Dixie Evans is absolutely clear: 'She has to have flair. She can be a good dancer, or whatever, but unless she can walk on to the stage thinking "Hey, I love you out there!", she won't be a great stripper. You have to really emote and give everything, because burlesque was the exaggeration of the real, and so you are this larger-than-life fantasy figure. It's not just about shaking what you've got – you have to tease in the most naughty and exciting way.'

This is the way it was once: a smiling all-American girl descending a glittering staircase above the heads of the men who watched, looking like an exotic bird, untouchable. In an act in which she used a swing, Lilli St Cyr was literally over the heads of her audience. 'It was great,' says Dixie. 'We were very much treated like movie stars, and I always tried to look very glamorous, even when I was just visiting my agent to pick up a paycheque. But it's over. Reality is that men won't wait that long for you to take off your clothes. Before, there was no question of men coming near enough to put money in your garter, but now, with TV and everything, people would rather see lap dancing, which is almost like the opposite of striptease.'

CHANGING TIMES

As television and the movies began to dominate the fantasy world of the mass audience, the wonderful, exotic creativity of striptease suffered. The burlesque queens could not compete with the wide-reaching allure of silver screen goddesses. Combined with attitudes of moral outrage, both in England and America, striptease was relegated to the back room, the private club, or the underground world of the sex industry. Debased and disregarded, it has reached the point where you can watch a woman take her clothes off on Friday night down the local pub - a sad demise of a once-vibrant art form.

Very little now remains of the old style of striptease, though some artists in America, such as Catherine de Lish at the Luna Park in Hollywood, are trying to revive the old atmosphere with elaborate sets and costumes. Striptease exists side by side with its less sophisticated sister, lap dancing. This trend, also imported from America, has nothing to do with the art of seductive teasing, but is more like a quick fix of a naked body, with no sense of temptation. Though the girls are beautiful and good dancers, there is a mechanical swiftness about lap dancing that destroys the erotic intent.

There are still some places where one might see glamorous nudity today. The Crazy Horse in Paris relaunched as a cabaret club in 1953, under the complete artistic control of director Alain Bernadine. His influence created a tightly choreographed striptease that featured a chorus line of beautiful girls. Now the show is professional, but it does not have the impact of the former flamboyant personalities who loved to seduce and tease.

At the Sunset Strip in London, each girl chooses a story that suits her personality. Routines range from simple striptease to elaborate stories involving vampires and virgins, schoolgirls, brides, fairies, devils and angels, nurses, secretaries and old-fashioned bondage. The light-hearted approach makes it fun and very sexy, and a refreshing change from the mechanics of lap dancing or the sordidness of video booths and boxes. Once an enjoyable, humorous and erotic performance art, striptease has changed unalterably to become just stripping. Without the craft and the creativity, performers look on their profession as merely a means to make money. The sexual revolution, changes in fashions, and the explosion of pornography on to the market has meant that audiences expect different things from striptease today - they expect full nudity as quickly as possible. Perhaps one of the only ways to reclaim the intimacy and eroticism of true striptease is to try it yourself.

Whirling to the centre of the stage she pulled off her skirt and stood in the centre clad only in her leopard-print panties and high heels. It was easy to see that some spirit possessed her. She swayed voluptuously under the light. She beat the big bass drum; she thumped the bongos with a wild uncontrollable delight. She was caught up in the blazing abandon of the rhythm. Her magnificent body seemed to shimmer before me. Perspiration dripped from my forehead. I opened my shirt collar. Her fiery dance continued, swirling and undulating. I felt myself grow dizzy. Slowly I staggered to my feet.

LAS VEGAS BUMP & GRIND, The Strip Record Label

144

Prepare your outfit, making it easy to peel off. The more you have on, the more exciting it is to take it off: stockings, high heels, a dress or a wrap, something to play with, a scarf…or a whip.

 Think exciting thoughts while you are getting ready.

Choose music that makes you feel sexy and inspires you.

Practise alone in front of a mirror. Watch yourself dancing and take off your clothes as slowly as possible. Play with a zip or tease with a strap. Let yourself move to the music and show yourself off.

During your performance, keep a distance between yourself and your audience - just far enough so that you are tantalizingly out of reach. Torment with the promise of your body, but keep it covered for as long as you can, especially the delicious parts. Enjoy yourself and watch the unbearable anticipation build up as you reveal a shoulder or a glimpse of thigh. Build up your performance to a crescendo, and then, as the music stops, turn off the lights and leave them begging for more.

148

Chapter 7 Sexuality

Why do certain images attract or affect us more than others?

That is the question that surrounds this chapter, which presents photographs and illustrations that have inspired us at Agent Provocateur. Some of the images are old favourites, others we came across while thinking about design ideas and still others are photographs of our lingerie that have appeared in the national and international press which we feel have captured our spirit. The images are all different - each one has something unique about it. The photographs by Helmut Newton, for example, though exquisitely arranged and stylized, have a disarming rawness that possesses you.

By contrast, the work of the eccentric Carlo Mollino gives the impression of spontaneity, as if he had no definite idea of what the finished image would look like, but that it was constantly developing in his mind's eye, like an accidental dream or fantasy.

His photographs were the result of a private obsession, which accounts for their amateur quality, though their secretive nature makes them all the more fascinating. Among the more surreal images depicted is the Ex Libris engraving of a garden of cocks, decorated in ribbons and flowers, encircling a radiant cunt. John Willie's blindfolded women, inspired by the work of René Gruau, are almost like modern graphics illustrations.

An important aspect of these images, as with any work of art that is captivating, is that you identify as much with the artist as with the work. Between you, the picture and its unseen creator exists a kind of affinity, as if you understand each other. There are elements in all the images that we find incredibly stimulating and that have influenced us, for reasons that are sometimes obvious and sometimes more obscure.

What is certain is that each image appeals to something personal within, and it is up to you to explore the ideas they offer.

Above: Randall's intrepid space explorers from the 1950s.

Opposite: Allen Jones' HATSTAND. 1969.

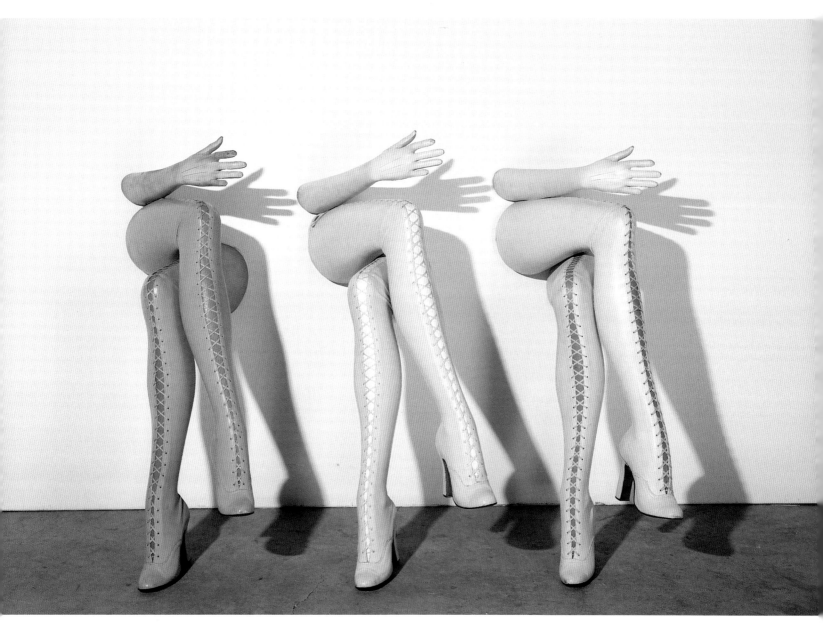

Above: SECRETARY by
Allen Jones. 1972.

158

Opposite: In the
Ladies' Room at
Regine's. Paris 1975.

Right: Inspired by René Gruau, John Willie created these images for the 1951 covers of **BIZARRE** magazine.

Opposite: Rituals of pleasure and worship – Carlo Mollino's sacrificial virgin.

163

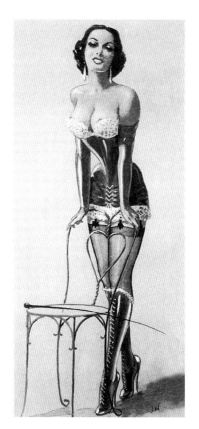

Above: Whips and wasp-waists – the art of John Willie.

Below: Pierre et Gilles' fantasy cowgirls.

RUSS MEYER'S "SUPER VIXENS

Meet Margot the Magnificent Superchick!

RUSS MEYER'S

up!

X

"Nobody pulls 'em in, nobody pushes 'em out like Margot!"

167

Opposite and above: Elmer Batters' little Indian and one of his contact sheets. Batters' single-minded vision of feet, legs and thighs encased in nylon and framed by suspenders has created some of the most powerfully erotic images ever seen.

Chapter 8

Agent Provocateur

OPENING AGENT PROVOCATEUR

At the beginning of December 1994, No.6 Broadwick Street threw open its doors to an unsuspecting public, whipping up an unprecedented media frenzy. The press was flooded with articles profiling the shop, praising the sexy lingerie and discussing the merits of the corset and the return of suspenders.

The response from customers was entirely enthusiastic. Women said things like 'Where have you been all my life' and 'I've been looking for something like this for years', or even 'This is my ultimate fantasy!'. Unfortunately, the response from our neighbours was not so positive. Violin-makers John and Arthur Beare, who own the property opposite, installed frosted glass in their windows to avoid the sight of Ferilyn, our mannequin, with her luscious upturned arse. More scandalous behaviour was in store when Naomi Campbell asked if she could be photographed in the shop. To the delight of passers-by, she brought Soho to a standstill as she performed a striptease in our window.

The windows have always caused controversy. The Christmas we opened, we featured an amusing six-foot penis-shaped Christmas tree, spurting cotton snow, which we made ourselves. An old lady who was passing by was so outraged that she called the police to demand that it be removed! We had to relocate the tree to the back of the shop to avoid being prosecuted under the eighteenth-century Obscene Displays Act, much to the disappointment of our customers – in particular one man who had driven over 100 miles with his girlfriend just to show her the window.

Other notable displays include our December 1996 window to celebrate the Order of the Garter,

with the words 'Honni soit qui mal y pense' (He who mocks shall be banished). The Order of the Garter commemorates an event at a ball in Calais in 1348, celebrating the British defeat of the town. Dancing with the Countess of Salisbury, with whom he was in love, King Edward III noticed that one of her garters had dropped to the floor. To save her dishonour and embarrassment, he picked up the garter and tied it around his own knee, much to the amusement of his Court. He retaliated with the famous saying, and created the Order – a blue velvet garter, worn on the left knee, for outstanding courage and chivalry.

Fashion Week 1995 was celebrated with a window showing our mannequin, Diane, hanging from a noose. She had a bag over her head and a sign around her neck, saying 'Fashion Week is Dead'. The other mannequin, Ferilyn, held the loose end of the rope and wore a sign on her bum that read 'This is Passion Week'.

MISS AGENT PROVOCATEUR

The shop and its windows continued to be used as a medium to communicate our spontaneous ideas. In turn, this attracted the attention of a host of creative people who wanted to become involved with Agent Provocateur. From this melting-pot grew the concept of creating a vehicle, in the form of a woman, who could communicate our ideas to a wider audience. Together with the national press, the search was launched for Miss Agent Provocateur – the girl who would represent the concepts behind the clothes, model new designs and be a spokesperson at upcoming events. She had to be charming, glamorous, curvy, independent and intelligent – someone with real star quality, whom everyone would love. From thousands of applications, a select few were chosen for the semi-finals. They had to answer three questions:

1) Who is your favourite political or cultural figure, and why?
2) What is the most outrageous thing you have ever done?
3) Why do you think you fit the Agent Provocateur image?

Twelve girls were chosen to go through to the finals, which were held in September of 1995 at the Connaught Rooms in Covent Garden.

London Fashion Week saw a controversial demonstration by the competition finalists, who paraded the streets outside the catwalk tents in their Agent Provocateur underwear, carrying banners with slogans reading 'Put the Passion back in Fashion', 'More S&M, Less M&S' and 'Come and see our Knickers'.

The girls were causing a serious traffic hazard as motorists, unable to believe their luck, concentrated on the provocative demonstration. Hearing the disturbance, journalists and photographers forgot about the catwalk shows and rushed outside to see what was going on. Nothing could stop these girls from completing their mission, not even the police, who eventually turned up to put an end to all the disruption. Demanding to know who was in charge of the abandoned group, the last thing the police expected was to be jumped on by the passionate protesters and smothered in kisses, while Joseph made a hasty getaway around the corner! The incident made the evening news.

MISS AGENT PROVOCATEUR PARTY

For the Agent Provocateur party, I found a huge, decaying Victorian ballroom, which I transformed into a brothel. Inside, in between masses of giant potted palms, I dotted enormous beds and gazebos, swimming in satin sheets. Each was home to a voluptuous whore, who gazed at the crowds all evening. For a centrepiece, I placed an old, white enamelled bath, complete with a gigantic camiknickered hooker manically bathing and scrubbing herself. The event was sponsored, so there was tons of free drink. By the end of the night, guests were rolling all over the beds and wallowing around in the bath with the old slag. Philip Sallon

The dress code for the two thousand guests was 'Strictly Brothel, Ballroom or Beauty Queen', which Philip personally checked at the door, refusing entry to anyone who was not suitably attired. First, the finalists had to 'boogie-woogie' to Jools Holland's band, and then each had five minutes to impress the judges with a performance of their choice. The panel, who included Vivienne Westwood and Cynthia Payne, were faced with magic tricks, a striptease, poetry readings and singing, and Roland Rivron compèred the event. A winner was eventually chosen, but we soon realized that it was impossible for any one girl to represent us: the concept is just too diverse. The Agent Provocateur exists inside every woman, just waiting for the opportunity to be correctly stimulated.

LOVE GROWS ON SEX
That's why Agent Provocateur has a lot to do with love. A new bond, provoking explosions of desire in the boredom of couple relationships, arming sex weapons to keep under skirts for self-defence - offence and laser guns for cupids at work. I'm sure that saved more families than any sermon in church. Agent Provocateur is fighting its own war to make people fall in love again, without any killing except for the common sense of decency. No shame in showing passions in a world that is falling asleep. Thank you guys. **FABIO NOVEMBRE**

I always wish I could go out in my Agent Provocateur underwear and nothing else. Maybe Serena and Joe should sell coats and macs and your outfit would be complete? KIM SION

The shoe equivalent of lingerie is my pair of Agent Provocateur moulded black five-inch stiletto mules. When I slip them on, I feel as though the heel goes right up through my body and into my heart giving me the desire and inclination to step out.
BELLA FREUD

I got married in a turquoise tulle bra and pants by Agent Provocateur, a gift from Joe and Serena. My dress was sheer and as I entered the church the vicar turned to his friend and said 'Fuck me! You can see her knickers!'. Thanks guys, it was a brilliant wedding. **CHARTY DURRANT**

Matching pink leopard shoes, bra and pants is the best suit I've ever had. You are quite the tabasco of the underworld - and I'm addicted to tabasco! Love from Cerys. **CERYS MATTHEWS**

Enough elegant pornography for titillation. ISABELLA BLOW

Agent Provocateur is definitely life enhancing! **JAMIE MACLEAN**

He was in Edinburgh, working. I was in London, lonely. One visit to Agent Provocateur, one plane ticket later, in the hotel room. One restaurant booked for a romantic reunion. He took a shower, I put on the AP kit, with stockings and heels under a trenchcoat. It was only out in the hotel corridor that I revealed the secret. We never made it to the restaurant. **LISA MARKWELL**

To me Agent Provocateur is the utopia of lingerie exotica and 'funderwear' delights! **KARL PLEWKA**

Perfect panties for playtime posing.
LUCINDA ALFORD

My favourite gift shop in London - always something to tickle your fancy. I get the heavy hint from my women friends when it comes to birthdays, anniversaries etc. Any excuse for them to empty my wallet. JUDY BLAME

I always like to wear Agent Provocateur when I'm doing my magic tricks. **YASMIN ESLAMI**, MISS AGENT PROVOCATEUR FINALIST

THE BRILLIANT THING ABOUT AGENT PROVOCATEUR KNICKERS IS THEY'RE EASY TO GET ON BUT EVEN EASIER TO GET OFF! **DENISE VAN OUTEN**

UNDERWEAR
UNDERWHERE?
UNDER ME TROUSERS
UNDER A SKIRT, A DRESS
UNDER A CHAIR
UNDER THE TABLE
UNDER THE BED
UNDER THE STAIRS
UNDER GROUND
OVERGROUND
OVER THERE
ANYWHERE
LOVELY LOVELY LINGERIE
BUT IT WON'T LINGER
LONG ON THEE
KATE MOSS

Agent Provocateur
RULES!! ELLEN VON UNWERTH

I can never look at lingerie from Agent Provocateur without experiencing a delicious frisson of anticipation - from the wearing and from the undoubted results which will then follow. **HILARY ALEXANDER**

Since Ossie Clark in the '60s, there's been a big dark gap, nothing...until Agent Provocateur opened. I just love it, the jewellery as well. Well done, it's right up my alley! **ANITA PALLENBERG**

Their knickers make the sun shine on a grey day.
YVONNE SPORRE

I got married in January and my ever-lovely mother made me a trousseau. In it, along with rose bath oil, a cotton nightdress, Cartier sunglasses and a bikini, was black tulle underwear, courtesy of Agent Provocateur. What can I say apart from it meant that my wedding night went off with a...well with a bang, not to put too fine a point on it. Where would we girls be without you? **SUSANNAH FRANKEL**

SOME MEN COME IN TO AGENT PROVOCATEUR WITH THE WRONG EXPECTATIONS OF THE SERVICES WE PROVIDE! MY FAVOURITE MALE CUSTOMERS ARE THE ONES WHO COME IN VERY NERVOUS AND LEAVE WITH A SMILE ON THEIR FACES, AND LADEN WITH BAGS. THEY OFTEN CALL A FEW DAYS LATER TO SAY HOW MUCH THEY AND THEIR PARTNER HAVE ENJOYED THEIR PURCHASES.
GINA GIBBONS,
MANAGERESS, AGENT PROVOCATEUR

I personally wouldn't buy underwear from anywhere else.
CHRIS SULLIVAN

About an hour after one of those intimate girlie phone conversations discussing the finer points of my sexy new boyfriend, a cycle courier arrived with a delivery. I immediately recognized the beautiful rose-pink box as Agent Provocateur. My friend Kim had very thoughfully sent over a little gift to guarantee success. How could tiny black glitter briefs with ties at the sides, which drop with one fell pull, be anything else? **KATY ENGLAND**

Never has mistress-wear and undies for lovers been so sensually displayed and so unashamedly provocative. **ROWAN PELLING**

My turquoise quarter-cup bra gives me bosoms. I bought it to wear underneath a see-through dress but I realized pretty quickly you can't wear those sorts of things in real life. So now it has other uses...my boyfriend loves it. **STELLA TENNANT**

My first pair was acquired after a fashion show. I found them on the floor under a chair in a very empty room. Thought I was very lucky and that this was a sign from above. **KARINA GIVARGISOFF**

Agent Provocateur have transformed the concept of underwear, taking a garment that was either unmentionable or not worth mentioning, and elevating bras and panties to a designer status. Always naughty, but nice. **VICKY SARGE**

Whenever you're wearing a pair of knickers, a G-string or a sexy bra, you know you're in for a very exciting night. For some reason, it always happens. **FRAN CUTLER**

Agent Provocateur-like fantasy island. The first example of Disneyland for adults. **ELIO FIORRUCCI**

When Agent Provocateur first lifted the shutters on their first boudoir boutique they crystallized my raison d'être as a shopping editor with their exquisite retail vision. A great shop should have character, spirited personalities and most importantly beautiful things to buy. Agent Provocateur gives us all of these things, and best of all an excuse to rifle through gorgeous knickers on a regular basis. TERRY BURGESS

Agent Provocateur is about the promise of sex, an exciting encounter. You go in there and you think about it. And thinking about it is good. Love is narcissism, and a nice pair of knickers is the nearest thing you can have to an orgasm that you can purchase on your credit card. **CHRISSEY ILEY**

The company's profile was rising, and in early 1995, BST-BDDP, the London advertising agency, approached Agent Provocateur with an idea for a 60-second cinema commercial.

TV SCRIPT

TITLE: Mannequin: Version: A

CLIENT: Agent Provocateur

LENGTH: 60 secs

DATE: 29 June 1995

Open on a close-up of a man's face. He's staring straight at us.

The camera quickly moves from his face round to the back of his head. We see that he is standing across the road and staring at the window of Agent Provocateur.

As he walks across the road we follow. SFX (special effects) footsteps behind him. He goes close to the window.

We cut to the scantily-clad mannequins posing on pieces of furniture.

We see one of the mannequin's faces suddenly come to life. She pouts, licks her lips and blows a kiss at our man.

We see him look at her in disbelief. He blinks as if he's dreaming.

Suddenly, the other mannequin turns and moves her breasts provocatively as she winks at him.

We then hear a smash and immediately SFX: smashing sound. An alarm starts to go off, ringing loudly!

We pull back to receive a full-length view from behind our man, who is still facing the window. He looks around, then quietly moves along.

As he moves away we see that there's a hole and a crack in the glass at waist level from his erection.

The camera zooms in closer.

We see type appear above the crack. It reads, SUPER:
AGENT PROVOCATEUR

Before its London-wide release, the commercial premiered at the adult Astral cinema in Soho in 1996. It went down so well that in 1998, in preparation for Valentine's day, we embarked on the creation of another cinematic adventure with ad agency BCD&P this time featuring Gina Bellman.

TV SCRIPT

CLIENT: Agent Provocateur

TITLE: PRISON

DATE: 28 September 1998

LENGTH: 60 secs

We open on the exterior shot of a men's prison. We cut inside to see a queue of women filing in to the visiting room.

We see one of the women, who's drop-dead gorgeous. She's wearing a leather raincoat, even though it's the middle of summer.

All eyes follow her as she walks, hips swaying, to a table and sits down opposite her boyfriend.

She then starts to act in a very provocative manner. She hitches up her coat and opens her legs.

Everyone else can see that she's wearing stockings.

She then starts to slowly undo her coat buttons. We catch a glimpse of wispy lace – it's obvious that she's wearing very little underneath.

All of this naturally has a startling effect on the other inmates. They sit open-mouthed, panting like dogs. The sexual tension hits boiling point as she gets up, strips off her coat and sits down wearing just a few pieces of silky lace and nothing else. The inmates hit meltdown. The man next to the woman lunges at her, and is punched by her boyfriend.

This sparks off a full-scale riot SFX: riot sounds, alarm bells, etc. Punches are thrown, chairs are smashed. From behind, we see the woman being led to safety by two prison officers.

We cut to her being ushered out of the prison gates. We then cut to the front view. We see that 'she' is in fact a 'he'. It's the boyfriend dressed in her underwear. He winks as he walks away to freedom.

The endline comes up: AGENT PROVOCATEUR. WHEN YOU WANT TO HAVE IT AWAY

Valentine's day is, of course, the most important date in the lover's diary, and in 1995 something truly different was added to the art of romance, with the launch of the stunning Precieux jewellery range. Designed in association with jewellers Erickson Beamon, these ingenious pieces completed the perfect lingerie ensemble. Drawing on a variety of influences, from Las Vegas showgirls to dominatrices and slaves, it was designed to add excitement to an outfit, offering a hint of subtle fetishism or a touch of high glamour. The pieces range from pussycat collars, perfect for daywear, to outrageous crystal-handled whips. One of the most beautiful yet notorious of the pieces is the handcuffs, covered in sparkling diamanté or crafted from fine silver mesh with a diamanté padlock.

In keeping with the idea of providing complete outfits, we heralded the coming of summer with the launch of the bikini range at The Sanctuary health club in London. Our notorious brand of eroticism was in full force as guests enjoyed The Bikini - a cocktail created especially for the event by London's premier barman, Dick Bradsell. The delightfully feminine Butterfly Bikini was shown off by girls lounging in inflatable orchids in the pool, while the biker chicks flaunted plunging cleavages, offset by a strategically placed skull and crossbones.

We indulged our taste for the exotic by inviting along some baby leopards, who cavorted with model Sophie Dahl, and an eight-foot python that happily took to pole-dancing with the girls. The party inspired photographer Ellen Von Unwerth to shoot models in Agent Provocateur's bikinis for ARENA magazine, with '...straight-ahead, disarming, sometimes downright disabling, glamour'.

All of these events obviously aroused a lot of interest, so to ease the frustration of our international and out-of-town devotees we launched an exclusive, limited-edition, mail-order catalogue in the form of playing cards. They caused a storm in the national press, and have since become collectors' items. Featuring 1990s pin-up girls with playful attitudes, the cards incorporated a classic collection of seductive lingerie, hosiery, shoes and jewellery. In 1998, a special set of playing cards was released to update the existing pack. Shot by Tim Brett Day, the cards feature sophisticated temptresses and serious voyeurs. In a departure from the naughty pin-up of the last set, the images focus more on an atmosphere of dark sensuality, inspired by the cult movie, PEEPING TOM. Eventually, the catalogue will comprise a full set of cards – perfect for playing strip poker! These images, as well as information on the company, can be accessed through the internet at www.agentprovocateur.com.

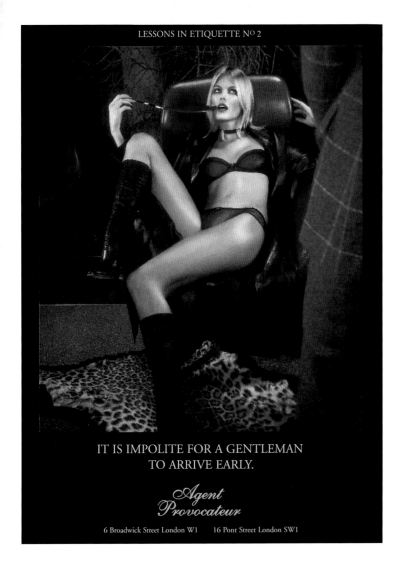

IT IS IMPOLITE FOR A GENTLEMAN
TO ARRIVE EARLY.

Agent
Provocateur

6 Broadwick Street London W1   16 Pont Street London SW1

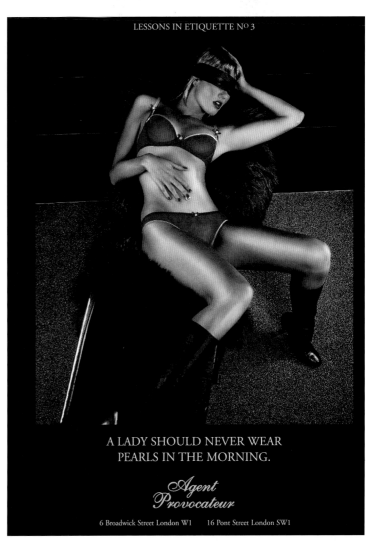

A LADY SHOULD NEVER WEAR
PEARLS IN THE MORNING.

Agent
Provocateur

6 Broadwick Street London W1   16 Pont Street London SW1

We decided to show our knickers to Knightsbridge. During December 1997, mysterious fly posters began to appear all over London, giving people some much-needed lessons in etiquette. Coupled with subversive imagery, the posters called attention to the fact that Agent Provocateur had moved a little closer to the inhabitants of polite society by opening their new shop in Pont Street, Knightsbridge. Downstairs, the shop has the added encouragement of an extra-special private boudoir, ensuring complete privacy for those who require it.

Agent Provocateur lingerie has turned up in all sorts of interesting places – from the pages of international magazines to exhibitions in fabric and textile museums worldwide. Lingerie from the collection was featured in the prestigious Victoria and Albert Museum exhibition of 1997, The Cutting Edge – 50 Years of British Fashion. Classic pieces from the collection are now on permanent display at the museum. Numerous television programmes have featured Agent Provocateur interiors, and our commercials have been shown at home and abroad to great acclaim. Added to this, many fashion designers have asked Agent Provocateur to participate in their seasonal catwalk shows.

Above, left and right: Fly poster campaign shot by Tim Bret Day, who quotes his main influence as Alfred Hitchcock.

'There are two sorts of women: those who care about the insides and those who care about the outs. Those who think expensive underwear is what they deserve and need – it's symbolic of their self-worth. And those other individuals who would put comfort before pleasure. Pleasure is never that simple. Pleasure, with all its complications, can come from Broadwick Street.'   Chrissey Iley

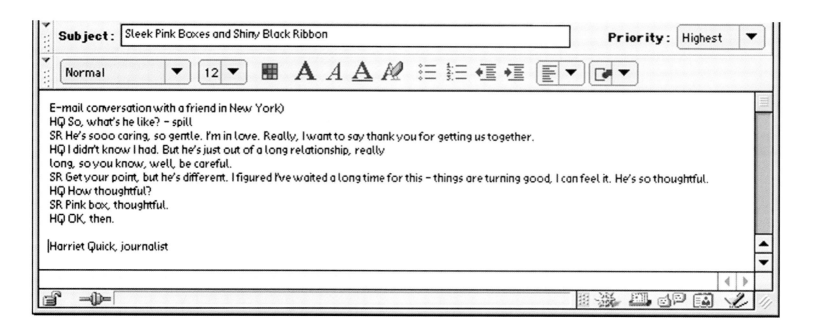

Normal   12

E-mail conversation with a friend in New York)
HQ So, what's he like? – spill
SR He's sooo caring, so gentle. I'm in love. Really, I want to say thank you for getting us together.
HQ I didn't know I had. But he's just out of a long relationship, really
long, so you know, well, be careful.
SR Get your point, but he's different. I figured I've waited a long time for this – things are turning good, I can feel it. He's so thoughtful.
HQ How thoughtful?
SR Pink box, thoughtful.
HQ OK, then.

Harriet Quick, journalist

The experience of Agent Provocateur lingerie begins in the shop and should continue when you get home, even before you put the lingerie on. The feeling of buying something special is enhanced by revealing to yourself what you have just bought, like giving yourself a present which has unlimited pleasure possibilities.

Untying the ribbon, removing the lid and unwrapping the tissue is like undressing yourself, and just as exciting. Leave the box at home, carry the bag again and see how many interested looks you get on the street, whether you are a man or a woman! In fact, the pink Agent Provocateur bag has been called 'the telltale trademark of the secret sex kitten', and has been photographed as much as the lingerie itself.

Interiors - No. 6 Broadwick Street

Ring the bell and enter a world of erotic intimacy... Agent Provocateur, Soho, is designed like a private boudoir with chinoiserie motifs. The colours are Empire red, black laquer and jade green. The artwork in the windows changes regularly, with timelessly classic displays, from Carlo Mollino's sacrificial virgin to contemporary nudes.

Interiors - No. 16 Pont Street

The light spacious interior of Agent Provocateur, Knightsbridge, is fresh and sexy. Inspired by eighteenth-century French interiors, the shop colours of Aubusson green, silver and bordeaux reflect the light that pours in through the huge windows. The wallpaper, patterned in fuchsia-pink and silver, was inspired by the traditional colours of the geisha girl, adding a subtle hint of Eastern eroticism.

The whole ambience of the shop was designed to reflect a more fragile sexuality than the smouldering intensity of Soho's interior. As you make your way downstairs, you are greeted by François Boucher's erotic work, LA PETITE MORPHÉE. Agent Provocateur has also become renowned for its sexy staff. Wearing uniforms designed by Vivienne Westwood, as well as high heels and stockings, they embody the ethos of Agent Provocateur, including all that is fine, original and erotic.

Shake It Baby

'I have been friends with Joe and Serena since they once lived near my home. Now, we are further entwined, with my wife making jewellery for them. My fondness for them is such that I have invented not one, but two, drinks in their honour. They remain very supportive of the cocktail experience.

So, early evening, if you find me hanging around Broadwick Street I am not trying to lasciviously ogle at their infamous window display that everyone, without fail, seems to stop and enjoy. It is more likely that I am watching the theatre of tourists, shoppers, clubbers and other Soho characters (even the local constabulary) who cannot quite manage to get past that particular shop front without breaking into a wicked smile. Oh, and I buy my underwear there, too.'

Dick Bradsell, London's premier barman

The Pontberry Martini

A light fruity martini which I served to celebrate the opening of the Pont Street shop. A suitable drink for parties where the guests are bound to drink to excess (this sums up most of the Agent Provocateur parties I have attended).

Into a shaker of ice, pour:
25 ml Smirnoff vodka
50 ml cranberry juice
3 tsps crème de mure (blackberry liqueur)
Shake thoroughly, strain into a cocktail glass and
garnish with a raspberry and a blackberry - one floats, one sinks.

The Bikini Martini

I created this cocktail for the party at The Sanctuary to launch Agent Provocateur's swimwear collection. It is rather strong but deceivingly smooth if made correctly.

Into a shaker of ice, pour:
50 ml Tanqueray gin
A splash of blue curaçao
A bigger splash of Archer's peach schnapps
A dash of orange bitters
Shake thoroughly and strain into a cocktail glass, into which a sizeable slice of lime has been squeezed.
Garnish with a lime wedge 'swimmer'.

BIBLIOGRAPHY

Anonymous, **English Woman's Domestic Magazine** (London, Ward Lock and Tyler, 1869). Excerpt on p 93.

Bataille, Georges, **The Story of the Eye** (London, Penguin, 1992). Excerpts on p 117 top, taken from pp 9-10; p 117 bottom, from p 33.

Christianson, Rupert, **Tales of the New Babylon: Paris in the Mid-Nineteenth Century** (London, Minerva, 1996). Excerpt on p 132 taken from p 61.

De La Haye, Amy, ed., **The Cutting Edge** (London, V&A Publications, 1996). Quote on p 48 taken from p 182.

The Erotic Review, 1 Maddox Street, London W1R 9WA.

Essex, Karen, and Swanson, James L, **Betty Page Life of a Pin-Up Legend** (Los Angeles, General Publishing Group, 1996).

Ewing, William E, **The Body: Photoworks of the Human Form** (London, Thames & Hudson, 1993).

Felix, Zdenek, **The Best of Helmut Newton** (New York, Thunder's Mouth Press, 1993). E Lévinas quote on p 35 taken from p 10; N Smolik quote on p 38 from p 4.

Fontanel, Beatrice, **Support and Seduction** (New York, Harry N Abrams Inc., 1997). Excerpt on p 51 taken from pp 52-3; quote on p 93 from p 48.

Friday, Nancy, ed., **Forbidden Flowers** (London, Random House, 1994). Excerpts on p 115 taken from p 100; p 119 from p 188.

— **My Secret Garden**, (London, Quartet Books Ltd, 1973).

Hawthorne, Rosemary, **Bras: A Private View**. (London, Souvenir Press, 1993).

— **Knickers: An Intimate Appraisal** (London, Souvenir Press, 1992). Excerpt on p 91 taken from pp33-4.

— **Stockings and Suspenders: A Quick Flash**.(London, Souvenir Press 1994).

Jarret, Lucinda, **Stripping in Time: A History of Erotic Dancing** (California, Pandora, 1997). Excerpts on p 117 taken from pp 78-9; p 130 from p 97.

Krell, Gene, **Vivienne Westwood** (London, Thames & Hudson, 1997). Excerpt on p 102 taken from p 18.

Marley, Diana, **Christian Dior** (London, Batsford, 1990).

Martignette, Charles G, and Louis K Meisel, eds., **The Great American Pin-up** (Germany, Taschen, 1996).

Néret, Gilles, **1000 Dessous: A History of Lingerie** (Germany, Taschen, 1998). Excerpt on p 57 taken from p 18.

Newton, June, ed., **Helmut Newton: Pola Women** (Germany, Schirmer/Mosel, 1995).

Nin, Anaïs, **Delta of Venus** (London, Penguin, 1978). Excerpts on p 72; excerpts on p 110 from p 215; p 115 from pp 154-5.

— **Little Birds**

Piselli, Stefano, and Riccardo Morrochi, eds., **The Art of John Willie**, Books I and II. (Florence, CB Nerbirni, 1995). Excerpt on p 30 taken from p 17, Book I.

— Piselli, Stefano, and Riccardo Morrochi, eds., **Exotic Gals** (Italy, Maggio, 1992). P de Cenzie quote on p 138 taken from p 7.

Price, David, **Cancan!** (London, Cygnus Arts, 1998). G Montorgeuil excerpt on p 134 taken from p 56.

Réage, Pauline, **The Story of O** (London, Corgi, 1995). Excerpts on p 48 taken from p 18; p 114 from pp 20-1.

Reyes, Alina, **Behind Closed Doors** (London, Phoenix, 1995). Excerpt on p 112 taken from pp 85-6.

Rice, Anne, **Beauty's Release** (New York, Warner, 1997).

— **Beauty's Punishment**. Excerpt on p 119 taken from pp 228-9.

Simon, Marie. **Fashion in Art** (London, Zwemmer,

Sinha, Indra, ed., **The Kama-Sutra** (London, Hamlyn, 1980). Excerpt from p 118 taken from p 54.

Waugh, Norah, **Corsets and Crinolines** (New York, Routledge, 1991). Excerpts on p 90, top, taken from p 45; p 90, bottom, from p 50 and 52; p 92 from p 129; p 93 from p 98.

Westheimer, Dr Ruth, ed., **Art and Arousal** (New York, Abbeville Press, 1993).

Willie, John, ed., **Bizarre** magazine. Quote on p 52 taken from 1946 edition.

The Gypsy Rose Lee quote on p 137 was found in 'The Costumer's Manifesto', a PHD thesis by Tara Maginnis, available on the worldwide web.

PICTURE CREDITS

Museum, Cologne, **Miss O'Murphy** 19

Daniel Brookman 181.

Carlton Books Ltd/Catherine Rowlands 130t.

Bob Carlos Clarke 182.

Jean Loup Charmet 94b.

Clifford Coffin/Condé Nast Publications Ltd 99.

Corbis/Everett 81, 98, 136/Historical Picture
   Archive 134.

Brian Connolly 180.

Paul de Cordon 142.

Jean-Philippe Delhomme 186b.

Robert Doisneau/Rapho/Network, **Dream
   Creatures**, 1952 111.

Sean Ellis/ styling: Helen Saddler, nails: Wendy
   Rowe at Marina Jones, model: Georgina, shot
   for **Dazed & Confused** no. 13, 62, 63.

Sean Ellis/ hair: Stephen Lacey at Streeters,
   model: Paula Thomas 70b.

et archive 16, 17, 18, 22t, 91.

Mary Evans Picture Library 94t.

Cecelia Fage 186.

Donna Francesca 33.

Leone Frolle 25/Stefano Piselli **The Newest
   Adventures of Sweet Gwendoline** 120.

Sean Gleason 75.

Ronald Grant Archive 5cr, 167r, 167l.

Huggy 189.

Hulton Getty 90, 97.

Lupita Jacob 105.

Serge Jacques 60, 64, 112, 157.

Drew Jarrett 173.

Allen Jones, **A New Perspective on Floors 1966**
   53, **Hat Stand 1969** 155, **Secretary 1972** 156.

Irving Klaw Studio 27tl, 27bl, 139, 141c.

Nick Knight/Condé Naste Publications Ltd 58t.

Kobal Collection 32, 34t, 41b, 51t, 73b, 116,
   130b, 137.

Magnum/Philippe Halsman 34b.

Milo Manara 11, 140b/141b.

Manasse 96.

Robert McGinnis © 1964 Danjaq, LLC and
   United Artists Corporation. All rights

reserved 41t.

Niall McInerney, courtesy of Vivienne
   Westwood, 103.

Magnum/Bruno Barbey 121.

Art, courtesy of Louis K Meisel Gallery 23br,
   23btr, 23btl, 23tr, 23bl, 23tl, 23abl, 23bcr,
   23tcr, 23abr, 23bcl, 154l, 154r.

Carlo Mollino © Fulvio Ferrari, Torino 161, 162.

Helmut Newton/TDR **Roselyne on Napoleon's
   Bed, Paris 1975** 20/2 **Study of Voyeurism,
   Los Angeles 1989** 38/39 **Tied up Torso,
   Ramatuelle 1980** 4 **Eva Wallen, publicity
   for Heineken beer, St Jean Cap Ferrat 1978**
   56, 122/123 **In the Ladies Room at Regines,
   Paris 1975** 159.

Nova/IPC International Syndication Ltd 5c,
   143, 148/149.

Paris-Hollywood French magazine no. 119
   November 1951 138.

Pierre & Gilles, courtesy of Yannick Morisot, **La
   Petite Marceline 1980** 72, **Viva Las Vegas –
   Las Vegas Pink Ladies 1994** 165b.

Rankin 10, 57.

Rex Features 35.

Bettina Rheims/Kehayoff, Munich 13.

Franck Roubaud 146.

D Ryan, courtesy of Vivienne Westwood 51, 104.

Jeanloup Sieff/Maconochie Photography **Corset,
   New York 1962** 50.

Julie Sleaford 6.

Eric Stanton 30r, 31, 113, 114.

John Stoddart 71, 168/169.

Tony Stone Images 118.

Steen Sundland/M.A.P. 45, 145.

Jurgen Teller/Z Photographic 54/55, 61, 69.

Donna Trope 14, 68, 79, 80.

Ellen Von Unwerth at Smile Management 48,
   65, 101, 106/107 and first published in **i-D**
   magazine September 1998.

Malcolm Venville 43.

Vin Mag Archive Limited 26tl, 26tcr, 27r,
   28, 52tl.

Roger Viollet 4l, 15, 22b, 133.

Warners Lingerie UK Ltd, **The Merry Widow
   Basque** 100.

Crena Watson 73t.

Ben Westwood 4c, 59, 66, 70t, 88.

John Willie 30l, 51br, 52bl, 52b, 160t, 160b,
   165r, 165l, 52tr.

Wally Wood 135.

Bunny Yeager 26bcr, 26bl, 158, 164.

Yevonde Archive, **The Machine Worker in
   Summer 1937** 4r, 85.

'Dear Millie' letter on page 95 by Keith de Dulin.

Frontispiece illustration: 'Time Bomb' Agent.
Provocateur girl by Charlotte Skeene-Catlin.

Gatefold: D Ryan, courtesy of Vivienne Westwood.

Endpapers: Borel, engraved by Ellium: The French
Aretino. In the style of Agostino Carracci.
Published in London, 1787

Front cover (model): Amy from Select
Back cover (model): Kina from Premier

We would also like to offer a very special thank
you to the following:
Serge Jacques, Teresa Roussin for all her kind
help in supplying photos from Brown & Bigelow
and Louis Meisel's Art Gallery in New York,
Leone Frollo, Tom Stanton (www.Stanton-
fetish.com PO Box 163, Gracie Station, New
York, NY10028), Bunny Yeager and Barbara
Tubaro at TDR for Helmut Newton.

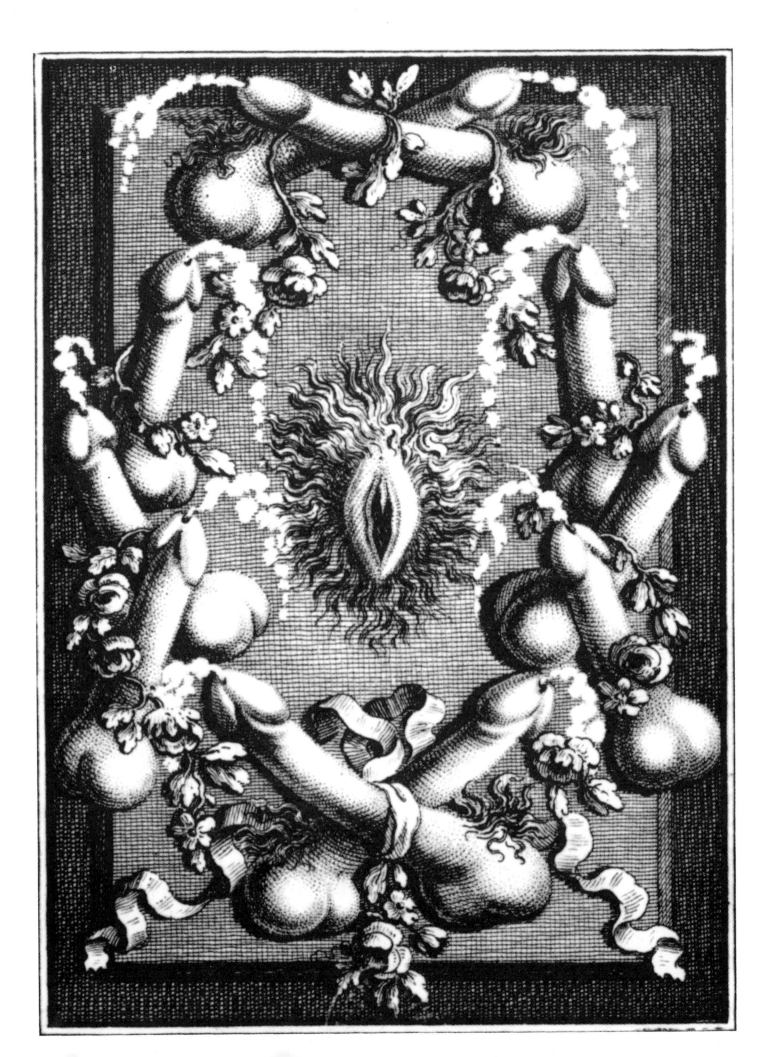